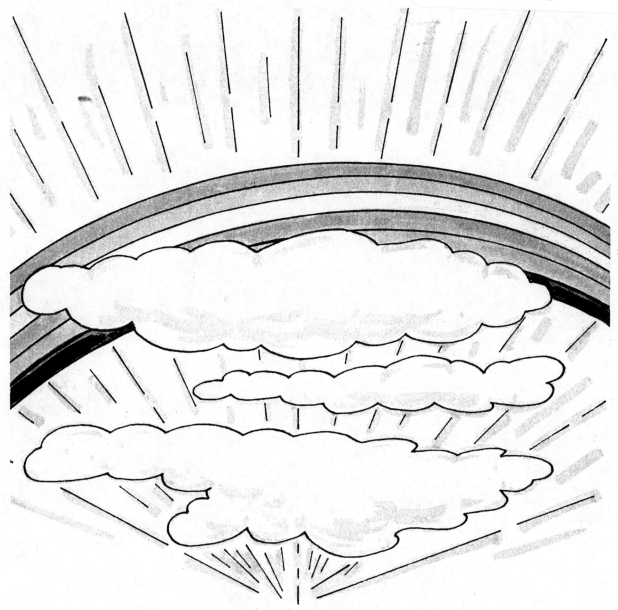

Principles and Applications
of
THE TWELVE UNIVERSAL LAWS

A Workbook for Children of All Ages

Written & Illustrated by Leia Stinnett

Principles and Applications
of
THE TWELVE UNIVERSAL LAWS

A Workbook for Children of All Ages

Written & Illustrated by Leia Stinnett

Other Books by Leia Stinnett:

A Circle of Angels
The Little Angel Books Series:
The Angel Told Me to Tell You Good-bye
The Bridges Between Two Worlds
Color Me One
Crystals R for Kids
Exploring the Chakras
Happy Feet
One Red Rose
When the Earth Was New
Where Is God?
Who's Afraid of the Dark?
All My Angel Friends (Coloring Book)

Cover art
by Leia Stinnett

ISBN 0-929385-81-0
Published by
Light Technology Publishing
P.O. Box 1526, Sedona, AZ 86339
(520) 282-6523

Printed by
MISSION
POSSIBLE
Commercial
Printing
P.O. Box 1495
Sedona, AZ 86339

DEDICATION

I dedicate this book first to Douglas, my beloved husband and companion, whose love, support and encouragement helped make this work possible. I am grateful for his wisdom and guidance, and for encouraging me to open my eyes and seek the greater truth that exists beyond this world of illusion.

To my children, Christina and Patrick, who helped me realize the importance of laying a solid spiritual foundation not only for my own children but for all the children of Earth, who will become the leaders of tomorrow's world. Only through God's love and by knowing the truth can they successfully complete their mission.

To my brothers and sisters of light — both those here on Earth in search of God, love and truth, and those not in body — who have lovingly encouraged me to create this book, this workbook is a reflection of my own awakening to truth. May it also serve to awaken each of you who are here on Earth to learn. And for those special angel helpers, may this work be a testimonial to your unselfish service to mankind.

To the great little beings born on the Earth now and to those who will come in the future, to each of you children who are wise beyond your years, who know only love, and whose mission is to bring divine love to a dying planet that can survive only through the reawakening of mankind to God, may this book serve as a guiding light to support that which you already know.

May this workbook serve as an instrument in helping each of us remember the truth of who we are and why we are really here. Through fully understanding and applying these laws of God in our daily lives we can each become again as little children. Our tears, sorrow, pain and suffering will be wiped away. We will again know LOVE.

PREFACE

The Twelve Universal Laws are God's laws, which were put into effect at the time of creation. Their purpose was to serve as guidelines for all aspects of creation. The instructions were simple: "Follow My laws, and live in peace, love, harmony, balance, health and abundance."

Through free will, mankind turned from God's laws and created its own laws. Mankind began to separate further from God, becoming more and more fascinated with the power of free will and creating a myriad of negative thought forms and experiences not of God. As a result, the Earth and all of creation began to exist in disharmony, chaos, confusion, disease.

Our mission is to assist in the awakening of mankind to truth and love, to merge separateness/duality with unity/oneness. We are here to help restore God's laws to the Earth. This workbook has been designed as a tool for better understanding and applying them. It is both a teaching and learning tool for all ages, to be used by teachers, parents and children.

The material might seem too detailed for younger children, compared to current children's literature. However, it is time we see our children as they really are — not as tiny, helpless beings who need our constant care, but as great, wise beings who have come to help raise the consciousness of the Earth to that of God.

As parents and teachers, we have a responsibility to better understand and apply these laws in our own lives, setting an example for our children to follow. By working with these laws and helping children work with them as well, the mission of light will be made easier.

To work with the younger children, you can create games, activities, exercises and meditations that they will understand. Children already know these laws; it is our responsibility to encourage them to follow them without becoming entangled in the laws mankind has designed.

None of us are happy with what we have created on this planet. We want change now. Some of us sit and wait for others to make changes, but change begins with each of us individually. As we stand in our own God-power, as we refuse to accept the past in the present moment, as we refuse to continue working with the old limitations, beliefs, structures, patterns and tapes, we will return to the truth and love from which we were each created. As we change, as we work with God's laws, we will bring to our planet more peace, love, balance and harmony. The Earth will again become as it was always intended to be. Now is the time.

TABLE OF CONTENTS

INTRODUCTION

In the beginning of the universe's creation, God carefully designed Twelve Universal Laws to govern the existence and experiences of all things created within the universe. These laws were established in close relationship to each other, overlapping in such a way that one law cannot stand alone without the other. Each law affects the other, and all work together as a unified whole for the common good of all.

The Twelve Universal Laws were specifically designed to keep the universe in order, operating in total balance and harmony. The laws are simple, easy to understand and work with. As we apply these laws each day in our life experiences, our life flows smoothly, like a gentle stream that moves ever onward. Through the correct application of these laws, we support and express balance and harmony in all that we think, say and do.

We are reminded that spiritual laws serve as a foundation upon which we can continually build from our lessons in life, a building process that leads us to a more complete understanding of our oneness with God. Spiritual laws serve as guideposts, offering sources of truth that we can believe in when all else seems to fail. In God there is only truth. And as Jesus reminds us, *truth will set us free!*

God created man and woman to live upon the Earth, presenting to each of them, as well as to the plant, animal and mineral kingdoms, a full understanding of the Twelve Universal Laws and how to use them in their daily life experiences. The laws were offered to assist mankind to maintain its connection to God while we experience the physical world and the lessons each has chosen to participate in.

God's plan for Earth was that through these spiritual laws, balance, harmony, peace, love, joy, health and prosperity would be a natural part of each of our lives on Earth. During our Earth school experience, spiritual laws would remind each of us that we were created in the divine image of God and that we have each been endowed with special gifts that allow us to experience balance, harmony, joy, peace, love, health and prosperity.

Along with the presentation of the Twelve Universal Laws, God also gave to each of us free will. Through free will each of us has choice. We can live in the physical world, experiencing all the beauty and love in all things and ever connected to the God that created us, knowing that everything we will ever need during our Earth stay shall be provided if we ask; or we can make our own rules outside of God's laws and experience the consequences.

Mankind has leaned more and more toward making up its own rules, believing that they could thereby create perfect order. After all, many people do not believe that God exists because they cannot prove His/Her existence through scientific means. Many people also believe that structure and control can bring peace, love and happiness. What do *you* think?

Through this decision to make their own laws, humans separated more and more from God, the God that lives within each of us. By doing this, we moved away from the universal laws that we had been given in the beginning of life on Earth, thus creating anything but balance and harmony. Can you think of ways mankind has interfered with the balance and harmony on Earth? How has this imbalance affected our standards of living? How have the imbalances affected our feelings of connectedness to God, to joy, peace and happiness?

As mankind continues to separate further from God, we have created disharmony, imbalance, disease and other dysfunctions in ourselves and in the plant, animal and mineral kingdoms, therefore in the Earth Mother herself. Mankind has created laws that judge, that discriminate in many ways, laws that create rebellion and unrest. We have created rules and regulations that separate us from one another, that set up boundaries, control and structure. Mankind's laws are anything but what God intended for us to live by.

In examining the laws established by people on the Earth, which ones seem unfair and unjust? How do these laws affect you personally? If you could change any of these laws, which ones would you change and how would you change them? How can God's spiritual laws be introduced once more to bring peace and harmony to the Earth?

We often feel that we are affected personally when society is not in balance and harmony with God's laws. Think for a moment. How many of our laws affect the entire community in which we live, or the entire world? For example, we can reflect on the dysfunctional attitudes, the beliefs, the control factor and the desire for power by a dictator and how this type of leader can affect a large group of people and the world at large. We too can affect our family and friends when we are out of balance. If we are angry, our angry energy can make others around us feel they want to move away. If we litter our roadways and others see us, we might influence them to do the same. On the other hand, if we are seen picking up the litter we could find others joining in the process. We set the example from our own center of balance. One person who makes a change can make a difference and affect many people. Think of dominoes falling down. If one falls against the other, the entire line will fall. If each one stands strong and tall, the line also stands strong and tall.

The purpose of this workbook is to introduce you to the Twelve Universal Laws that God presented to mankind at the beginning of creation on Earth and in the universe. The laws affect all things everywhere in all of God's creations. You will learn the definition of each law and through various meditations and exercises can familiarize yourself with the functions of each law and its application in your daily life. This book can be used by your entire family. Many of the exercises and explanations are designed for small children and teens as well as adults.

The lessons and exercises are simple; however, their impact on your life can be powerful. Work with the laws daily. Record the changes that happen by using the laws. Remember that *all is energy* (*the first law*). Our thoughts are energy and they affect everyone and everything they come in contact with. You *can* make a difference.

Take your place in line in a changing world, a world that shall reflect "as above, so below" or "on Earth as it is in Heaven."

First

Second

Third

1 • THE LAW OF ENERGY

Fourth

This law states that all is energy. God created the universe and all things within it as part of a vast ocean of vibrating molecules or atoms — energy. The energy of God is in all things. This energy is love, perfection, oneness, balance, harmony, peace, well-being, abundance and goodness. Because we were created from the energy of God, we also inherited these God-qualities of goodness.

Each of us lives and breathes in this sea of vibrating energy. Energy is always moving, always changing form. We bring energy from the universe into our bodies through our breath, the food we eat, the water we drink and from the sunlight we absorb into our bodies. We bring energy into our bodies from the Earth, for the Earth has her own energy that she gladly shares with each of us, an energy that loves, nurtures and "grounds" us into this experience. We use this energy to stay alive, to keep our heart beating and our lungs bringing oxygen into our bodies. We use energy to do everything we do, from reading and meditating, to running and jumping. We use energy in our thinking processes, in healing our bodies, in speaking and doing.

MEDITATION ON CREATION

To better understand the different forms of energy, let's meditate on the creation of our universe. Pay close attention to the many types of energy God utilized in creating the universe, the Earth and all living things.

For this meditation, sit in a chair or lie on the floor. If you have a group participating with you, sit or lie in a circle on the floor. The circle will help the energy flow in a loving way from one person to another, just as God's energy flows from the source of all life to each of us, to all things.

Place your hands on your thighs, close your eyes and begin to breathe very slowly, relaxing your body with each breath, coming into your center and grounding the energy into the Earth, feeling connected now to the universe and the Earth.

In the beginning there was God. God is, always has been and always will be. And God is **ENERGY.** *Imagine this energy of God in any way you choose. God is* **LOVE.** *Let that love be in your heart now. Feel God as love. Feel God's love for you.*

In the beginning God created the heavens and the Earth. The Earth was without form and empty. Darkness was everywhere, and in the darkness the spirit or energy of God moved. Be in that darkness. Feel the darkness, the nothingness. Feel the energy of God, the love of God moving through the darkness.

And God spoke, "Let there be **LIGHT.***" Thus, through God's spoken word was created the energy of* **SOUND,** *a divine sound. Hear God's words as energy; feel those words as energy.*

As God spoke, "Let there be light," there was light. Feel the energy of light.

God separated day from night and designed the heavens and the Earth. Feel the energy of the heavens. Feel the energy of the Earth. Notice how each feels different —the vast openness of the heavens; the warm, nurturing energy of the Earth Mother. Feel the heavens as having no form, as flowing, moving energy. Feel the Earth as solid, dense, having form.

And God said, "Let the waters under the heavens be gathered together in one place, and let the dry land appear." Feel the energy of the great oceans, the rivers and streams. Feel the energy of the land.

God then called forth the grass, trees and plants. Feel the energy of these living things. In your imagination feel the energy of all that God created, all the different energies.

And God created the stars, the Sun and Moon and all the planets. Let yourself expand outward into the great universe. Feel the energy of the stars, the Sun. Feel the energy of the Moon. The Sun is a powerful, life-giving energy. The Moon is gentle, loving, as nurturing as the Earth herself. The Sun represents masculine energy; the Moon, feminine energy.

And God created the seasons of change: Spring was created to bring new growth to the Earth.

Summer was created to assist in the growth of plants to maturity. Fall would bring the harvest of the summer's growth. Winter would be a time to rest, to be renewed. Feel the energy of each of the seasons. Feel the energy in growth. Feel the energy in rest.

God created all the creatures of the Earth and sky. And God created people in His/Her own image — male and female, balance and polarity. God created balance in all things — darkness and light, day and night, the Sun and Moon, land and sea, male and female — balance. Feel the energy of this balance in all things. Feel your oneness, your connectedness with all that God created.

And God breathed life into man and man became a living soul. Feel the energy of God's breath. Feel the energy of creation complete.

Let your eyes open as you feel ready and be present in this moment.

THE ENERGY OF THOUGHT

Creation began with a thought. God was all alone in the vastness of space. He/She looked about this vast, empty space and thought how wonderful it would be to create the universe and all the living things. *Thought was the energy that preceded creation.*

We each were created in a very unique way, apart from other creatures. Part of our thought process as human beings originates in what we call our CONSCIOUS MIND. This is the mind we use in our daily experiences at home, school, work or play. This is the thinking part of us that deals with immediate physical needs. We think about what we are going to wear to school, what we are going to eat for breakfast and so on.

The SUBCONSCIOUS MIND is like a hidden part of us. It lies deep within our mind, where information or thought forms are stored to use at a later time. When we need the information, it is made readily available.

For example, someone teaches us how to thread a needle. We do not plan on sewing, but we have learned how to do this step in the sewing process. We store the experience in our subconscious mind. One day a friend loses a button on her blouse. She asks us to help her thread the needle. From our subconscious comes the information we need.

The SUPERCONSCIOUS MIND, or the mind of our Higher Self, is the part of us that is ever connected to God through our energy bodies and that is always linked to the mind of God. Thus anytime we have a question or a problem of any type, we can go into a relaxed state of meditation and ask God to offer an answer to our situation. The answer comes as a thought or knowingness from God.

Thought is a natural process of living. Through the energy of thought we learn. The moment God thought about what He/She wanted to create, it was created. We are a part of God, one with God, one with the mind of God. Thus we must come to realize that we too can create with the energy of thought. One of God's universal laws presented in this workbook reminds us that *what we think, we create!*

Think about something special that you would like to have. Perhaps you would like to have an ice cream cone. You think about how that ice cream cone would taste and smell, what it would look like, what flavor and color you would like. You imagine this cone in your hand. This cone becomes so real you can taste it. Suddenly your friend invites you along for a special treat — he's taking you to the ice cream parlor. By thinking about what you want, you create through energy the very thing you are wanting.

Giving thought to something means giving it energy. Therefore if you think loving thoughts about someone, that person receives the energy you send as love and responds in a loving way. The person may smile or give you a warm hug. The opposite, however, is true if you send angry thoughts. Your life becomes whatever you think it should be, or whatever you accept from other people who tell you how to live your life. Remember, you do have a choice.

Send loving, positive thoughts to yourself, to friends and family. Think about how special your home and community, the entire Earth and all the Earth's living things are. Send loving energy to all things everywhere. Your loving energy can make other people, plants and animals feel much better. You will be happier in return.

EXPLORING THE ENERGY OF SOUND

When God said, "Let there be light," He/She was sending out into the universe the vibration of SOUND. **Sound is energy.** Different sounds are created from a different amount of energy moving at a different speed through the universe.

When we speak, we are creating an energy of sound. The sound travels on waves of energy from our mouth to another person's ears, where the waves of energy are heard as sounds or words by the brain. Some sound is healing and creates harmony, balance, and centeredness. Other sounds affect our energy field in such a way as to create disharmony, imbalance or disease; they make us nervous and irritable. Can you imagine how it might feel to live in a construction yard, near an airport or by railroad tracks? Can you imagine how it might feel to live in the country on a farm with no other homes within several miles of your house? How might each setting feel?

Exercise

Play some loud music, a tape of train whistles, construction work, automobile horns or the sounds of traffic, loud voices, screaming from a television program and so on. If you do not have a tape of sounds such as these, you can record them on a blank tape from television programs or from areas in your neighborhood.

While the tape is playing, sit in a chair with your spine straight. If a group is participating, sit in a circle in chairs or on the floor. Close your eyes and focus your attention on the sounds you are hearing.

How does the sound feel in your body? How does it affect the way you feel? Do you feel calm and relaxed? Do you feel nervous, irritable or angry? Do you want to put your hands over your ears or run away?

Now play a tape of the sounds of nature – water, birds singing, a soft rain, the wind. How do the sounds of nature make you feel? It is believed that the sounds of nature can be very healing to the human mind and body. How do you feel when you are out in nature? Have you ever felt hurt, angry or sad, then after sitting in or walking out in nature felt much better?

It is important to protect yourself from sounds that create imbalance and disharmony in your life, sounds that do not feel comfortable and pleasing to you. Loud sounds in particular create imbalance. Some sounds create an energy that can make you feel more and more separate from God. Some sounds can give you a headache or pain in some part of your body.

It is important to maintain good health, balance and harmony in your life. Listen to gentle, soft and loving sounds that are in harmony with who you truly are — a part of God.

EXPLORING THE ENERGY OF LIGHT

Light is energy. Light is the essence of God. God is light. Light is an energy we are all a part of. Where there is any form of darkness, we instinctively know that by turning on a light, the darkness goes away. It is said that darkness is merely an absence of light and that where there is light there can be no darkness.

Darkness often causes fear in many of us. We are afraid because we cannot see with our physical eyes what is in the darkness. We do not know what to expect in the darkness. The following activity will help you clear this type of fear.

Exercise

Sit in a quiet place. Breathe deeply and close your eyes. Focus on something you are afraid of. Now imagine God's light coming down through the opening of your head. Focus this light on your fear. Direct a beam of love in this light. See the light and love dissolve the fear, like a big, dark cloud dissolving away. Keep sending this light and love until all you feel and see is the light and love.

God is within each of us as a light energy. When we call upon this God-light energy within us, we feel safe and protected. We surround ourselves in God's light as a huge bubble or cocoon. We know that God's love and protection is inside this bubble and that all things we do not wish to feel are outside. Nothing can come into God's light that is not of love and light. The true essence of who we are as a soul is light energy. We are light.

In healing, we can focus God's light as an energy of healing directly to the part of our body that is in pain or hurt in some way. Since all is energy, that part of us that is out of balance or in pain is also energy. It is interesting to note that through the energy of thought we can actually create an illness or energy block in our body. Thus, through the energy of thought and the energy of light, we can bring our body back into balance. Our body is energy; and energy is constantly moving and changing. Thus, our body's energy system can be changed by the use of energy, moving the unwanted energy out and replacing it with loving, positive energy.

The next time you have a headache, earache, stomachache or other pain or illness, sit quietly. Imagine the area of pain or discomfort and energy that is not in balance with your God-energy. Focus on God's light and direct that light to the painful area. And see the light as a ray that brings balance and harmony to the affected area. Affirm to yourself that your body is in perfect balance. If you concentrate any energy at all on the pain, the pain will increase and remain in your body. Think of the area as healed, and so it will be. Even the most severe illnesses on Earth today can be healed with a conscious thought, desire and belief in divine perfection, that since mankind was created in God's image of perfection, none of us have to be sick or in pain, or suffer in any way.

EXPLORING THE ENERGY OF FORM

Form is energy. When God created the Earth, stars, the Sun, the Moon, planets, plants, animals and people, He/She gave to each a particular shape, or form. Energy that has such form as those things living on Earth are said to be dense in vibration; they move or vibrate at a very slow rate of speed. These forms of energy can be perceived with the physical senses of sight, hearing, touch, tasting and smelling.

Energy can change form from a solid to vapor (air), just as we can change in our form from a dense physical body to total light in our spiritual body. Let's do an experiment.

Exercise to See Change in Form

Take a cube of ice and place it on the stove in a saucepan. Look at the ice. The ice has form. It has shape and is solid. As we turn on the heat, the ice begins to melt. It becomes a different form of energy — liquid. Liquid energy moves freely. It still has a shape, but it is less dense.

As more heat is applied to the water, it becomes steam. The dense energy of the ice cube has now taken a new form — air. Thus in this experiment you can see how form can become formless as the vibration is changed. The steam rises into the air, and is transparent light.

If this vapor were to be trapped in a special container as the water evaporated, when it cooled it would form droplets of water in the bottom of the pan, and we could once again freeze the water, and once again we would have a dense, solid form.

We can compare our own body to the ice. The physical body can be related to the ice cube. The etheric/emotional body can be compared to the liquid form of the ice, and the mental and spiritual bodies can be related to the air, or vapor.

The human body consists of four types of energy, each vibrating at a different rate and each serving a different purpose: the PHYSICAL BODY has eyes to see with, ears to hear with, a nose to smell with, a mouth and tongue to taste with, and a body that is capable of feeling or sensing the outside world. The physical body is dense; it has form; it is heavy. The body has taken this dense form in order to experience the Earth lessons.

The ETHERIC/EMOTIONAL BODY is an energy body we can sense with our hands and our intuition. We can "see" it with our mind's eye. This part of us is called the **aura**, which reflects various colors that reflect whatever emotion we are feeling in that moment.

We live in a sea of vibrating energy. **All is energy**. Energy flows in and out of our bodies through our breath, and through seven major energy centers, or **chakras**.

Each chakra center is responsible for maintaining a certain balance in our emotional state regarding different aspects of our physical and spiritual experiences. For example, the Root Chakra at the base of our spine is responsible for our needs in surviving on Earth, for keeping us grounded to the Earth. The Second Chakra deals with our feelings, our ability to feel energy outside ourselves and deal with it intuitively. This center helps us stay balanced sexually, allowing us to work from our center, where the male and female energies are joined as one. Each of us has both male and female energies, and we must learn to balance them to be in balance with God and God's universe.

The Third Chakra deals with our ability to create, or manifest, what we need on Earth. This center assists us to stand in our own power, not letting others direct our lives. It is also where we feel the emotions that result from the things that seem to disempower us — anger, helplessness, fear and so on. The Fourth Chakra deals with the emotions of anger, sadness, joy, happiness, love, guilt and so on. Here is where we can feel love flowing through us. As this center comes into greater balance, we learn to shower ourselves and all living things with unconditional love more and more in our lives.

The Fifth Chakra is located at the base of our throat and assists us to communicate. When we are in balance, we speak truth to all those with whom we communicate. We do not hold words back out of fear of being wrong or of being punished for saying the wrong thing.

The Sixth Chakra is our mind's eye and is responsible for our "seeing" things, our "clear seeing." It shows us things our eyes can't see because they are perhaps many miles away or are not in solid form or are hidden in some way.

The Crown, or Seventh Chakra, is our connection to our Higher Self and to God. Through this center we feel God's knowingness. When we use our intuition, we do not need to ask advice of anyone outside of ourselves. We are able to know what we need to know and act on it, realizing that God is guiding us in all ways and knowing that we are safe in making such choices. Through this center, when it is in balance, we continue to learn through God rather than through listening to our friends who often do not know what is best for us. God is always here for us, no matter what the situation.

The colors of the aura are reflected in the etheric/emotional body from each of the chakra centers. Because our emotions change second by second, our aura changes just as often. Thus when we have our aura "read" by someone, we might find that in one moment blue is present and in the next moment the person is seeing yellow, orange or red. Our aura reflects what we are feeling in the moment.

Exercise to See Aura Colors

Sit quietly, eyes closed. Rub the palms of your hand together to sensitize your hands. Now hold your palm about six inches from the front of your body. Let a color come into your mind's eye or your knowingness. What color do you see or sense? See how many colors you can sense in your energy body. Think of something that makes you angry. How do the colors change?

*In reading the colors, **red** refers to love, passion, vitality or a lot of energy. It can also relate to anger. **Orange** represents balance in male and female energies, creativity, the ability to feel energy openly. **Yellow** is the color of intelligence, being very bright, happy. **Green** is the color of balance and harmony; **pink** relates to love. **Light blue** refers to open communication with the* *physical and spiritual worlds.* **Indigo**, *or dark blue, is the color of the mind's eye. It refers to our intuition and how well we are using this gift at the present time, our ability to "know" things.* **Violet** *is a color of spiritual awareness, a closeness to God and the angels.*

For another person to read your aura, simply stand in front of a blank wall. The person reading the colors should take a deep breath, relax the body and eyes. The colors will begin to show in the form of energy around the head and shoulders. Write down the colors you see. Notice how they change each time you have your aura read.

The energy body molds itself to the shape of the physical body. It is like the water that comes from melted ice cubes. It has form, but it is not solid. This body can be felt with your physical hands with a little practice.

Exercise to Feel the Aura's Energy

For this exercise choose a friend or family member to work with you. Sit on the floor or in a chair, about two feet apart from one another. Face each other. One of you should sit quietly, hands on thighs or in lap. The other should rub his or her hands together to create more sensitivity or the ability to feel energy.

When a tingling sensation is felt by the person rubbing hands together, hold one hand about six feet from the front of the other person's body and move it up, down, and all around.

Can you feel a hot or cool sensation? A tingling energy? Something that feels like a wall? This is your partner's energy field, the edge of the energy body called the aura.

Have your partner move to one end of the room and stand with eyes closed. Beginning from the other end of the room, walk toward your partner, asking him/her to say "stop" when feeling your energy field. As you enter your partner's energy field, your partner will feel your energy touching his/her field, bringing an awareness that someone is moving closer than might be comfortable. This is our warning that someone is in our energy field, and it gives us an opportunity to greet them lovingly or move away from them, whatever we intuitively feel.

It is through our energy field that we sense things in our environment. We can feel it when there is someone around us who is angry or happy. We know when there is something uncomfortable so that we can move away, or when there is something we enjoy so that we can participate. Our energy body helps us sense energies that are or are not helpful to our spiritual growth and well-being.

The etheric/emotional body is fluid: it moves and changes. It does not have density. It vibrates at a much higher rate than the physical body; however, it vibrates at a rate that still allows us to sense it with our physical senses as well as our other "extra" senses.

The MENTAL BODY consists of what we are thinking. It is an energy body of thoughts. We cannot sense this body in a physical way; yet it has a form, in the sense that we can travel in this body to wherever we give thought.

Exercise in Mental Travel

Think of a place you really want to visit. Close your eyes. Imagine this place. See the place, feel the place, hear the sounds of this place. Smell the different scents of this place and taste the place. Make the picture as real in your mind as you can. The mental body is actually traveling to where you are directing it with your mind.

This body extends farther from your physical body and cannot be seen or sensed with the physical body. It is much more difficult to see or sense with the intuition as well. Disease or negative experiences begin in this energy body. Thus it is important to think positive, loving thoughts to keep healthy this body as well as the physical and emotional bodies.

The SPIRITUAL BODY is pure light. It resonates with the energy of God. The spiritual body is always one with God and thus expresses the love, all-knowingness, all-wisdom of God. This body vibrates at a very fast rate and cannot be sensed with the physical or etheric bodies except through meditation or out-of-body experiences. Scientists have weighed persons who are preparing to pass over in death and find that their weight differs by a few ounces after they pass over, signaling to the research teams that the soul does exist, that the soul does have weight.

EXPLORING GROUP ENERGY

We each are here on Earth to work together, to focus on creating balance and harmony in our world, where all people can share equally and live happily, as God intended. When Earth and mankind were created, God intended for us to live without separation, judgment or discrimination.

When we are balanced within ourselves, listening to our inner guidance and following the spiritual laws God created for us, we find our life experiences full of joy. When we are happy, we radiate that happiness to others in the form of energy. If we are angry, we also send that energy out to others. Anger creates more anger. Joy creates more joy. We always have a choice.

Exercise in Moving Energy

This activity is more effective if there are at least six people standing in the circle of energy. Remember that a circle represents an unbroken flow of energy with no beginning and no end. The circle represents the energy of God and each of us in God as one spiritual family.

Bring God's light down through the top of your head. Bring the energy down and fill your entire body with God's light. Bring the energy into your heart and expand it until all that you feel is this powerful energy of light. Change this energy now to a feeling of love. Energy can be changed instantly by your thought from one feeling to another, from one vibration to another, from light to love, or from love to light.

Fill your heart with love. Move this love down from your heart into your right arm and hand. Pass the love into the left hand of the person on your right. Move the energy all around the circle. As this energy is moved from person to person around the circle, soon the whole circle begins to radiate an energy of love.

Increase the energy, the feeling of love. Increase the energy until you feel so much love that it fills the entire room. Now drop hands. What happens to the love energy? What happens to the energy in the room? What happens to the energy of the circle? The energy from one person to the other?

Join hands. Focus on increasing the feeling of love all around the circle. What happens to the flow of love energy? How do you feel?

As one person counts to three, every second person in the circle from the counter on drops hands and moves backward out of the circle. What happens to the loving energy now? What happens to the energy when we get out of balance and harmony with God's loving energy with other people, with the Wholeness, with God?

This exercise teaches the importance of working with God's spiritual laws as opposed to the laws established by people. When we are in balance and in harmony with God, we are happy, healthy, joyful and loving. When we are out of balance, we find ourselves unhappy, angry, confused, separate and alone.

OTHER FORMS OF ENERGY

There are many forms of energy that we use in our daily life experiences, energy that helps make our life simpler and more enjoyable. Much of the energy we need in our life experience comes from natural sources at Earth's surface — sunlight, water and wind. Using natural forms of energy keeps our Earth environment clean and balanced. Taking elements from inside the Earth's body creates imbalance and problems for future generations.

The direct energy from sunlight can be used to heat and cool our homes and offices, to operate specifically designed automobiles and equipment. Solar batteries can be purchased in specially designed wristwatches, clocks and toys. Solar-operated ovens, water heaters and so forth have been developed.

Swift-running water passes through large generators at power plants to produce electricity. Heat from deep within the Earth often creates water hot enough to produce energy for personal and manufacturing needs.

Wind can be harnessed in various ways to produce power. There are many farms and manufacturing plants across the nation that have set up windmills to pump water or create electrical power when the wind turns the vanes or sails on top of the mill.

Fossil fuels such as oil, natural gas and coal are extracted from the Earth and used to operate equipment, and to heat our homes and office buildings. Unfortunately, this type of energy can be used up and its use is a source of serious pollution of our water, air and soil. Thus it is becoming more and more important for us to rely on natural methods of providing constantly renewed energy such as the sunlight, wind and water to provide electricity and power for our everyday use.

Nuclear power plants have been built in many parts of the world. These plants also use elements from beneath the earth, and although they produce a great amount of power, they also create toxic atomic waste that can remain active for millions of years, polluting the soil and water supplies, making the Earth very unsafe. Wherever the waste materials are deposited, there is danger of transforming the entire area used for this purpose into a wasteland.

REALITY VS. ILLUSION

In the beginning we existed within the energy of God. We were each created from the great light and love of God. As directed by God's thought at creation, we separated from God's light to become individual lights. We took on a physical body to learn in the density of the Earth school.

Through the energy of thought we became an individual soul light. Yet we are ever connected to God's love and light, to the all-knowing, all-seeing, all-present God energy.

God said, "This light of Mine shall now be separated, yet ever connected, as individual souls take on physical form to learn in the Earth school the importance of following My laws." God noted that as each soul learns upon the Earth, God also learns through the process, through the connectedness.

God gave to mankind the energy of sound — a voice and the ability to hear and speak. The energy of sound, as it was presented to mankind, was to teach us that God can speak to us and through us, that as each of us learns to listen inside ourselves, we can hear God.

And God created form — shapes, density, matter — and free will, a test for each of us living on Earth. As long as we followed God's laws we would experience free will as God's will and learn that even in such physical density, God's truth could still be heard and followed. The task was to maintain oneness with God in a world that offered the temptation of physical "things," a world that began to believe "there is no God," a world that moved further from the very source that created it. After all, who could believe in something that did not have form? We became obsessed with form, with the beauty of the physical body and the physical world, with how many possessions we could obtain for ourselves. We became obsessed with the *me* instead of the *we*.

In moving further from God, people created many illusions for themselves, illusions that have moved them away from spiritual law. Some of these illusions include:
- "I am separate from God. God is "up there" and we are "down here."
- "I have to work hard and 'earn' everything I need or want."
- "Power is demonstrated by how many things I own and how important I make others believe I am."
- "By controlling others, I have power. The more I control and manipulate other people,

the more things I will have and the more powerful I will be. I will then have respect. People will look up to me."
- "I have no control over my future. Everything is preplanned. I am a helpless and vulnerable victim of circumstance."
- "Other people have made me think this way. It is everyone else's fault that I am not happy."
- "Suffering is a natural part of the life experience."
- "If I do something wrong, God will punish me."
- And there are many, many more such illusions.

Thus God gave to each of us spiritual laws to follow while mastering this physical world of matter and illusion. We were given the opportunity to use our cocreating abilities to learn and grow spiritually for the good of the whole rather than for the individual self. In the beginning, mankind experienced God within itself and in all things. Balance and harmony existed in the world.

Through the free-will experiment, we were given choice. We could follow God's laws and live happy, healthy, joyful and abundant lives, or we could make up our own laws and experience the consequences of separateness. Through the choice of separateness and by the misuse of the universal energies and laws, mankind created an imbalance on Earth, one that is causing serious problems for the world and her people today. We see air pollution, pollution of the water and soil and destruction of plant and animal life. We see disease, war, chaos, confusion, pain and suffering. It appears that people have forgotten all about God's laws. In the process of making their own rules, people have begun to destroy the very Earth that sustains their lives.

BALANCING THE SCALES

Many people feel they cannot make a difference in the imbalances on Earth. On the chart above, the column on the left lists the qualities God created as part of the Twelve Universal Laws. The column on the right indicates some situations that have resulted from our misuse of God's laws. The center column offers an exercise for you to list the situations you are creating in your life now. Are you creating happiness, love and joy? Are you working to bring about more positive changes on Earth? Or are you helping to create discomfort, disharmony and unhealthy situations for yourself or the Earth?

How can you bring those qualities you see within yourself more into alignment with God's qualities of love, perfection, balance, and oneness? For example, if you are playing loud music, how might you change the energy by playing soft, spiritual music? How might you learn to work cooperatively with people and get others to work more closely with one another?

BALANCING THE SCALES BEGINS WITH ME

GOD CREATED	I AM CREATING	MISUSE OF ENERGY HAS CREATED
Sound/tones	_____ _____	Noise pollution
Light/faith	_____ _____	Darkness/fear
Divine love	_____ _____	Selfishness/no love
Perfection	_____ _____	Disease, disharmony, dysfunction, confusion
Balance/harmony	_____ _____	Too much, too little, haves, have nots
We/ours as one	_____ _____	Me, mine as separate
Oneness	_____ _____	Separateness
_____	_____ _____	_____
_____	_____ _____	_____
_____	_____ _____	_____
_____	_____ _____	_____

What do you feel you are creating in your own life? Are those things you are creating bringing you happiness and joy or discomfort and disharmony? List those aspects you feel you are creating. How do they relate to the consciousness on Earth today? How do they relate to the divine Mind, God's Mind?

THE ENERGY OF MONEY

Of all the material goods and possessions mankind has created on Earth as part of its life experience, money is one form that has brought considerable conflict to us. Money is the means of exchange humans have chosen to use on the Earth plane to purchase whatever is needed to bring comfort to their experience. Money has been the cause of conflict, greed, power struggles, even death.

Sometimes known as "green energy," money was never intended to be hoarded by one person at the expense of another. Money is an energy that was intended to be part of mankind's lesson in learning to share with one another. There is an energy created by sharing money that causes whatever we give out to return to us tenfold, or ten times the amount we give.

If you loan a dollar to a friend in need because you love this friend and want *from your heart* to help him, you will receive back at least $10 or more as a gift or in some other form. We are encouraged to tithe or share a portion of the money we earn or receive, offering this money to others in need. In exchange we receive ten times what we give. When we do not give from our heart, we block the energy and cannot receive.

Money is energy. Energy is thought. Thus whatever we think about money becomes true for us. If we fear lack or not having enough money, then we create this lack. If, however, we give lovingly to others, knowing we will always have plenty for ourselves, we create abundance. The more money we give lovingly and willingly, without holding energy about having it paid back, the more money we receive in return. It is one of the universal laws.

EXPLORING THE ENERGY OF OTHER LIVING THINGS

We are not the only living things with this special sensing device, this energy field. All living things have an energy field, or aura. When we sensitize our hands we can feel the energy field around plants, animals, insects, even rocks and minerals.

Each living thing has a different energy field; some vibrate very rapidly because they have a lot of energy, and others vibrate more slowly. When we have a lot of energy, we feel vibrant, lively and happy. When our energy level is low, we are tired or we do not feel well. We move more slowly and are not as excited about playing with our friends. We are also more vulnerable to energies that are not helpful to us.

Exercise to Receive and Send Healing/Love Energy

For this exercise you will need to have two different plants. One plant should be very green and healthy. The other plant should be one that looks a little droopy.

Rub your hands together until you feel a tingling sensation in your palms. Holding the palm side of your hand about two inches from its leaves, first feel the energy of the healthy-looking plant, then feel the energy of the drooping plant. Compare the energies of the two plants. How can you change the energy of the droopy plant to make it feel more like the healthy plant?

Bring down a special healing from God through the top of your head at the Crown Chakra and out into your hands. This is special love energy from God. Love is the most powerful energy of the universe and can help all living things come into balance and feel more energized.

As this energy comes down into your hands, feel your hands tingle just as they did when you rubbed them together. Feel the warmth. Now place your hands on the plant or on the plant's container. Let this special love energy flow from God through you and into the plant.

After a few moments, feel the energies of the two plants. Does the energy feel more balanced? Do the energies of the two plants feel somewhat alike? Give more love to the plant. Test the energy the following day.

Practice feeling the energy of animals, insects and rocks. How do the energies feel different?

Practice with your family and friends. Feel each other's energy body. How do you differ from each other? What do you feel?

Try sending energy into your own body when you feel tired or sick. Place your hands anywhere on your body, where you are drawn to place your hands. Let the energy flow from God through you and into your body. After a short time check how you feel. Do you have more energy? Do you feel better?

AFFIRMATION: As I sit quietly I find the inner peace within myself that is You. I feel my oneness, my wholeness, my balance with All That Is. You are in me and I am in You. God and I are one.

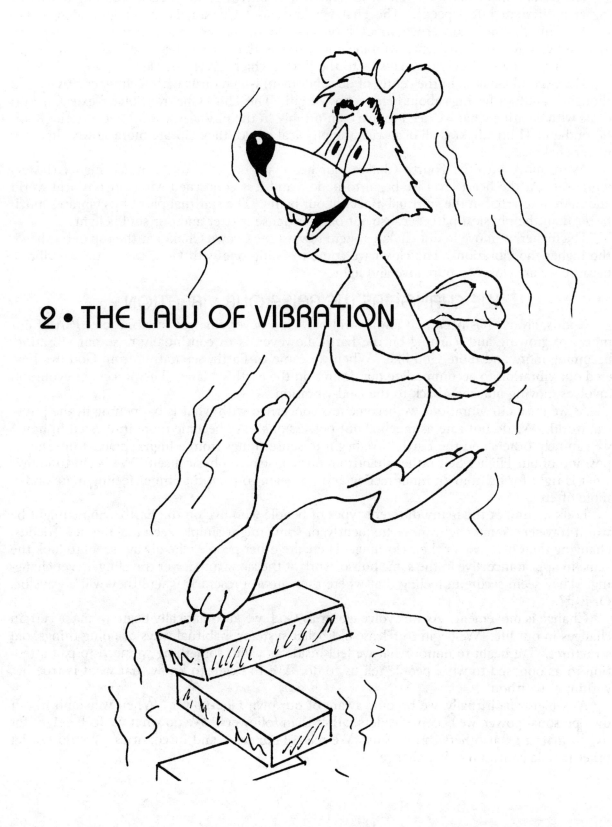

2 • THE LAW OF VIBRATION

In the previous lesson we demonstrated that we live in a sea of vibrating energy consisting of moving particles of atoms and molecules. Everything in the universe vibrates at a different rate. Dense objects such as rocks, mountains and planets vibrate at a very slow rate. Light, on the other hand, vibrates very fast. With our physical eyes we can see through light, but we cannot see through a rock or a mountain or the Earth.

The human body houses seven major chakras, or energy centers, each spinning or vibrating at a different rate (speed). The First Chakra (Root Chakra) keeps us grounded to the Earth. This chakra is concerned about survival — food, shelter, water, clothes and people to love and care for us. This center vibrates more slowly than others because it is the one energy center that most closely connects us to the Earth, which is very dense

The Second Chakra, in the center of our abdomen, which deals with feeling, creativity and thoughts, and our feelings about being a boy or girl. The Third Chakra (Solar Plexus Chakra) deals with creating what we need to live comfortably in the physical world. Because the Root, Second and Third Chakras all deal with the physical world, they vibrate more slowly than our upper chakras.

As we move into the Fourth Chakra, our heart, we begin to find a much higher (faster) vibration. At the heart level we begin to be less and less concerned with our physical world and more interested in the spiritual aspect of our being. The spiritual part of us vibrates much faster than the physical part, because our body is dense matter and our soul is light.

The higher we move in our chakra system toward the Crown Chakra at the top of our head, the higher the vibration. The closer we come to being one with God, the faster we vibrate because we are closer to pure love and light.

WE CHANGE AS WE RAISE OUR VIBRATION

God is, always has been and always will be. God never changes in vibration. Part of our proess of growing and learning on the Earth, however, is to continually raise our vibration, becoming more and more God-like. When we came to Earth, separating from God, we lowered our vibration to accommodate our desires on the earthly plane. The process of evolution involves moving ourselves back to the God-vibration.

As we raise our vibrations we become less concerned with what is happening in the physical world. We do not care as much about possessions. We become more interested in how we can help others and the Earth. We begin to sense things from a higher place, from the position of our Higher Self rather than from our conscious, physical self. We begin to know what is right for us from an inner feeling and we begin to trust that inner feeling more and more often.

Look around at the many different types of people who live on the Earth. Some might be world travelers, some might move frequently, or some might simply keep making new friends, changing their hairstyle or their clothing. There are other people who always seem to look the same in appearance, live in the same house, work at the same job, never traveling, never changing. They seem secure in feeling that where they are at present is where they will always be. Or is it?

Change is movement. As we evolve closer to God, we automatically begin to make certain changes in our life. We begin to release old belief systems, habitual ways of doing things, old structures. We begin to honor what we feel inside as valid, something we need to pay attention to as opposed to what people tell us to do. We to begin to know that what is true lies within, not without.

As we grow spiritually, we become aware of our own God-power. When we stand in our own personal power, we become leaders rather than followers. We do what we feel is right for us, no matter what others think of us. We release our fears and insecurities. We do not let other people control us. We change.

Let's look at some of the types of changes that people make in their lives.

• Moving whether from house to house, city to city, across the nation or even to another country. Moving can be very difficult if we are leaving close friends and family behind. Sometimes it is difficult to leave behind the home and neighborhood where we grew up because it feels so comfortable.

• Changing schools or jobs can be very difficult because there are always new faces and new ways of doing things that we have to adjust to. A new routine is not always easy to adapt to unless we are open to change.

• Friends can leave through disagreement or because one of you moves far away. As we grow spiritually, we tend to change friends very rapidly, and sometimes it is difficult to understand why a certain friend is no longer with us. As old friends move out of our space, our lesson is to be open to meet new, more like-minded friends. Thus we will have assistance from new friends in areas we do not yet understand.

• Death, whether it be a family member or friend, can, change our lives in a way that is difficult to deal with, especially if we are not comfortable with the dying process. When we understand that death is merely a transition from one life experience to another, we can more readily accept what we feel as a loss. Death teaches us another lesson about change: Nothing stays the same; everything changes as it moves from birth to rebirth.

• Dietary changes can be a real challenge whether because of health situations or a desire to nourish the body better. As we become adolescents we often become more involved with our outer appearance and looking "good." Thus weight maintenance seems to be a constant focus. As we change our diet, our body responds with change. Good, healthy foods create a strong, healthy body with more vitality. We feel and look better. *We* change.

• Illness in the family, whether it is our own or that of a family member or friend can create some challenges. It can help to view illness as a time when the body can heal itself and rest, a time to change from one focus to another. Illness can also help us reflect on old patterns or beliefs we need to release and heal. When we are ill, our vibration is much weaker than when we are healthy. It is at this time we need more rest, more time to meditate, more time to reflect and change.

• New ways of thinking that we adopt as we grow spiritually change the ways in which we speak and act. Many of our old habits fall away and we become more centered and balanced.

As we begin to change and evolve in our consciousness, all aspects of our being are affected. The physical body begins to change its appearance. It might look younger and younger, radiating more health and vitality. The body reflects positive change in the way it moves and relates to others. Or the body might go through periods where it needs more rest, different foods and more water than usual. Perhaps it even craves certain vitamins and minerals to keep it strong and healthy. Listen to the body. The body really does talk.

Our emotional body takes on a different picture as well. We begin to feel more loving and compassionate toward others, even when they are not very nice to us. We find we are no longer afraid or insecure. We no longer worry about what is going to happen tomorrow. We do not feel so emotionally involved in the physical world. Thus we do not tend to get as upset about situations and people as we used to.

Our mental body begins to think in a more positive, loving way. It no longer seems to let negative thoughts control the actions. We begin to operate from the Higher Mind, from God. As we begin to focus on positive, loving thoughts, we project these thoughts to others.

Our spiritual body raises in vibration as we grow spiritually. The more we operate from the consciousness of the Higher Self, the greater is our light; thus our vibration is raised as well.

RESISTANCE TO CHANGE

If change is so great, why don't we allow change to take place in our life without resistance?

• An old pattern or belief can be buried so deeply within us that we have no awareness that it is an obstacle to our growth. It might take several similar situations happening to us before we can become aware of the pattern and let it go.

The universe has a unique way of bringing the same people into our lives who display the very issues we are working on or need to work on. For example, we look about at our friends and notice that some of them seem to be very controlling or angry. As we examine ourselves, we might find that we too are trying to control everything in our life or that we are also angry about something. We refer to this type of situation as the *mirror*. In other words, someone reflects to us exactly what we need to work on within ourselves. As soon as we complete this lesson, these friends will leave our life experience. We will then begin to draw more loving people into our life as we become more loving ourselves.

• A fear of change because we don't know what to expect if we do change. What will happen to us? How will we act? How will we look? Many of us are afraid of the future, the unknown.

Spiritually speaking, we often refer to the unknown as a vast, dark abyss, a void, something we cannot see into to determine how deep or expansive this darkness might be. It is like entering a cavern without a light, moving carefully into the darkness, with the mind moving from one fear to another — fear of failing, fear of death, fear of being lost and so on. It is the same scenario in life experiences. We fear change because we do not know what is on the other side of this vast darkness. Will we get hurt? Will we lose everything we have gained up to this point? Will we lose all our friends and be alone in the world? Will others disapprove of us as we change? Will we no longer be acceptable to our families or society?

The universe demands that we grow. To change is to grow. To eliminate the fear of change, we must learn to trust in God. This is not easy for us because we are unable to trust what we cannot see or feel. We must remember that God is a part of us just as we are a part of God. Therefore, God is ever with us and supportive of our changes. As we surrender to change and allow change to take place in our lives, we are able to release the past experiences that keep us from growing spiritually and move into a place where we begin to create the kind of life we want to have for ourselves and our family.

• Resistance to accepting new things in our life because we are comfortable in the security of what we are experiencing. We rationalize, "Why do something new when I know what I can expect from the way it is now?"

As we grow spiritually, we become aware that the material things of the physical world are not as important as we thought they were. As we perceive the situation, we begin to see things taken away from us or things not working out for us in a given area. We feel that we must be doing something wrong. What is taking place, in fact, is a nudging by the universe to move on, to allow room for growth by being willing to change and accept the new thoughts, feelings and ideas coming into our awareness. The longer we resist what we are being encouraged to do by universal energies, the more difficulties we will have to face. It is the way the universe tells us it is time to move on, time to grow. Our response can move us easily and effortlessly into a place that does work for us, or into a place where we continue to grow more and more unhappy. We have free will. We have the choice.

• A feeling or belief that the situation will simply take care of itself without our personal involvement.

How many times do we ignore signals that tell us we need to make a change in our lives. We ignore these signals, believing that the situation will simply heal itself without our having to do anything. For example, we are very unhappy with a certain friendship. The friend is constantly taking advantage of us in some way. We feel that if we tell this friend how we really feel, he/she will be angry, hurt us in some way or abandon us.

The universe will not let such a situation rest. There is always the loving encouragement to love through the experience we have chosen for ourselves. We must learn that we are the masters of our own experiences. If we want a situation to change, we must create what we want with our thoughts, actions and deeds. When we complete the lesson, we move on quickly and happily into a new experience.

We might not even be aware of our resistance to change, but our avoidance behaviors say it all. Can you personally relate to any of the following?

- We change the subject because we don't want to talk about it. We resist and avoid.
- We leave the room (another form of avoidance). We feel that if we are not there to face an issue and listen to what is being said, we will not have to deal with it. Sooner or later, however, we will have to do so. The longer we put it off, the more complicated the experiences will become that surround the lesson.
- To ignore a situation we do something else like watch television, listen to tapes or read a book. We somehow believe that by doing something else the situation will just go away. Wrong! The situation will be there until we do something to change it.
- We sometimes get sick because we know we can plead illness to avoid something. However, being sick offers the perfect opportunity for the mind to reflect on a situation that needs change. This is a good time to look at the entire picture, select the perfect solution and make the appropriate change.
- We procrastinate. We put off something we're anxious about and do other, less important things to avoid making the change. One thing the universe does not allow is putting off important lessons. We can try, but we will not succeed. Change is part of the lesson we have come to Earth to learn.

We often *justify* our resistance to change by *assuming things about other people.* Do any of the following situations sound familiar?

"My parents just wouldn't understand." (You can substitute friends, relationships and so on.)

"I don't want others to talk about me or think badly of me."

"None of my friends do that."

"My situation is different."

"It's not important. I don't want to bother them."

Then we continue our resistance to change by letting some of our belief systems about ourselves get in the way. For example:

"It's just not right for me."

"It's too difficult."

"I'm not that kind of person."

"It wouldn't work for me — I'm different from everyone else."

"It doesn't follow my spiritual practices/beliefs."

"It's too much work."

Do any of these beliefs sound familiar to you? Do you have any favorites you would like to make note of? If so, write them down and pay attention to how these beliefs may be preventing you from making positive changes in your life.

A very common practice for many of us is to *give our power away* to others in our effort to avoid change.

"God wouldn't approve."

"It's against my spiritual beliefs/practices."

"I'm waiting for them to tell me it's okay."

"I don't have the right teacher."

"I can't do it in this place."

"*They* have to change *first*."
"I will do it *after* I get what I want."
"It's too hard to understand."

We postpone or put off change by tricking ourselves into believing:
"I'll do it later. I can't think about it right now."
"I don't have time right now. I'll do it later when I have time."
"I have too much to do."
"I will do it next year."

We also use *denial* that there is any need for change.
"There is nothing wrong with me. What good would it do to change?"
"If I ignore it, the situation will simply go away."

We each know from our own life experiences and involvement with change that none of these beliefs are true or practical. The excuses only prolong what we know we have to do.

Fear is one of the strongest reasons we resist change. Fear is an absence of light, an absence of faith and trust. Here are some of the most common fears:
"I might fail."
"My friends might make fun of me or abandon me."
"I don't know enough."
"I'm afraid to talk about it. Someone might get angry with me or think I'm crazy."
"Who knows what might happen to me if I do that."
"I might get hurt."
"I might get punished if I do that."

Let's talk about each of these briefly. First, *there is no failure unless we fail to try.* All we can ever do, all that is ever expected of us from our Creator, is that we do our best. Each experience is a learning process; there is no right or wrong way to do something. If we do something that does not work out, we are encouraged to try something new. This is the way we learn. Lessons are the reasons we came to live on Earth, because they provide growth.

When we make a change in our life, the change first affects us and then others. Many, many people do not like to make changes, nor do they like to see their friends or families make changes, either. Thus friends may attempt to talk us out of making changes in our lives, telling us that if we do a particular thing, they will not be our friend any longer. They might even ridicule us, hurting our feelings.

Oftentimes we believe that if we make a change, it will not meet with the approval of our family and friends. We often feel that we will be punished for making a change, whether it is something positive or not. We need to realize that any change we are encouraged to make by our own feelings is a change that can only be helpful to us in our growth. We must realize that punishment often comes from another person's refusal to see that change is in our best interest, or from their belief that the change will have a detrimental effect on them or others. Parents can sometimes be overprotective and overcontrolling, not wanting us to move out on our own without their approval.

It is important to realize that we are responsible for ourselves and our own happiness. We cannot change anyone else, no matter how hard we try. It is important to realize that other people do not have power over us unless we give them that power, even our parents. We must learn to communicate lovingly to others what we feel. In this way we can help them understand our feelings and what we hope to achieve through the changes we want to make. We are not here on Earth to create conflicts, but to lovingly help one another grow and prosper in God's love and light.

Exercise to Experience Nonchange

What would it be like if nothing on Earth ever changed — the seasons, the climate, the plants, the environment? What would it be like if *we* never changed? Through this exercise, we can experience more fully how important the Law of Vibration (the Law of Change) is to Earth and all of creation.

Close your eyes. Breathe deeply, letting your body relax more and more. Relax completely, focusing on your breath. Let your mind be empty of all thoughts. If any thought comes into your mind, simply let it float on out, or put it into an imaginary pink balloon and send it on its way out into the universe.

Look around at the world. You see trees, plants and flowers; you see mountains and streams. The sky is blue, very blue. There is one cloud in the sky that is white and fluffy. The cloud seems to be stationary, not moving.

There is no breeze. The air is still and warm. The sun is shining brightly as birds sit in a tree and sing.

You are lying under the tree, watching this picture that never changes. You see the same picture over and over every day of your life. There are no seasons. There is no wind, rain or snow. There are no other clouds, no night, no other people or living things in this picture. Nothing ever changes. It is the same picture every day of your life.

You never change. You do not get any older. You wear the same clothing every day. You lie under the tree and gaze at the same picture over and over. Nothing EVER changes. How do you feel?

Change brings the seasons, the day and the night, the Sun and the Moon. Change takes each of us from infancy to adulthood and to maturity, to rebirth. Change allows each of us to experience various lessons, each lesson helping us evolve back to the energy that is God. We are here to learn to work appropriately with the energies of love, truth, change, freedom, clarity, balance, oneness and knowingness. We learn these qualities as we grow and change through our life lessons.

MAKING CHANGES EASIER

There are many ways in which we each can learn to accept and promote change within ourselves easily and effortlessly.

First, we must **recognize within ourselves the need for change** and understand why that change needs to take place.

When we feel that our life is no longer working as it should, we need to stop what we are doing and focus on what we feel inside. What do we feel we need to do now? Next we can think of ways in which we can implement a change and then examine what might occur in our life if we make that change. For example: We feel we need to tell a certain friend that we are no longer going to let him/her take advantage of us. We feel that we have been taken advantage of over and over, and now we feel there is nothing to be gained from continuing the relationship except more problems. Looking at the situation, we feel that as we let this friend know we are going to move on, the friend might get very angry and strike us, might call us names or even attempt to make us change our minds. For instance, the friend might say something about going to other mutual friends and telling them some of our personal confidences.

To release this friend, we must be ready to let him/her go from our life, knowing that the friend no longer serves us in any positive way. We do not want to hold onto any ill feelings, but we wish to simply tell them it is time for us to move on into other experiences. Then it is important to realize that this friend might feel hurt and rejected by our decision and strike out at us from this hurtful place rather than because he/she really means to make us feel bad. We must be ready to deal with whatever is thrown at us.

We must realize that by releasing this friend and the experience, we will be prepared to draw into our life experience more loving friends who do not attempt to control us. Thus we can make room in our life for more happy events. As we understand the outcome and allow the shift to occur, we begin to feel better about "going with the flow" and allowing changes to occur in our life.

Second, when we realize that we need to change a thought, action or emotion, we can **create a positive thought about what we want** to develop in our life. We make an affirmation, a positive statement that replaces a negative feeling, thought or action. For example, we want to lose weight. Instead of beating ourselves up over and over thinking about how fat we are, we simply state to ourselves out loud, "I am the perfect weight" or "I now weigh . . . (whatever you wish to weigh)" and think lovingly about yourself as the pounds drop to the desired weight.

Try making a chart of "Affirmations of Positive Thoughts and Feelings" that you wish to bring into your life experience. Place this chart or the different statements wherever you feel you can best see it and use it. You can place them on the refrigerator door, your mirror, on the dashboard of the car — anywhere they will be most visible so you can give them energy to create the situation you want in your life. Positive statements and positive beliefs bring positive experiences into our life.

Third, we can **visualize what we want to create.** Once we understand what we are learning or have learned from an experience and are ready to move on to something new, imagine a picture of what you want to create, see or feel or know it as real, give it positive energy, telling the universe that this is what you are now creating for yourself because you deserve it and you are worth it. When something is not working, we have the power to change it with our thoughts and actions. We are not helpless on Earth. The longer you wait to change what you are not happy about, the more unhappy you will become.

Fourth, when we want to make changes in our lives, we can **get quiet and meditate on the situation** and what we can do to make our lives happier. Sit quietly. Breathe and relax the body. Imagine yourself moving higher and higher, up into the sky, beyond the clouds and upward. Feel golden light around you, the light that is your Higher Self, your soul, that part of you ever connected to God, to spirit.

In this higher space it is easier to realize that the change you need to make is a positive change to benefit your soul's evolution. Ask your Higher Self, the angels of light or God to assist you to make the necessary changes easily and effortlessly.

Fifth, we can **use the breath to release unwanted feelings and bring in positive feelings.** Sit quietly where you will not be disturbed. Focus your mind on what you wish to change within yourself. Breathe in the light and love of God. Surround yourself in this light and love. Feel that energy throughout your body. As you breathe out, let go of those feelings and thoughts you wish to release or change. See them no longer serving you. Thank them for bringing you the necessary lessons and release them, for they are no longer helping you grow.

Breathe out the old, breathe in the new. Allow the new energy to move into your body, to help you feel stronger, happier.

As we each allow room for change and growth in our life, we begin to work more closely with the God-energy within us and our life will begin to reflect loving, joyful experiences. We find it easier to complete things at home, school or work. We will find our friends more like us, not wanting to control and manipulate us, but loving us unconditionally and sharing experiences that are fun and meaningful. As we allow change, our vibration is altered to a higher vibration. We move closer to God on our evolutionary path.

AFFIRMATION: As I grow in the light of God, I realize and accept change as a positive aspect of my evolution as a soul. I am flexible and open to change. I look forward to new lessons and new experiences.

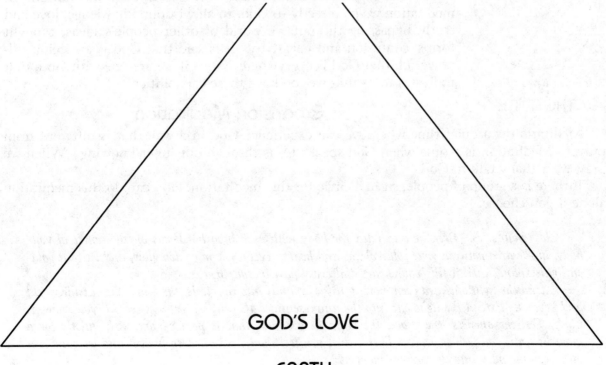

UNIVERSE

GOD'S LOVE

3 • THE LAW OF AS ABOVE, SO BELOW

GOD'S LOVE

EARTH

We begin to work with the Law of As Above, So Below by developing a deeper, more complete understanding of who we are. To know who we are, we need to understand what is going on in our life, our environment and the world around us. In this way we begin to see more clearly those areas we need to correct.

As we fully understand our personal needs and inner desires, we can eliminate discord in our lives, thus experiencing peace and harmony. In this lesson we will be examining the symbols and messages God sends to us that help us see more clearly what changes we each need to make to create more balance and harmony in our lives on Earth and in our relationship with God and all life.

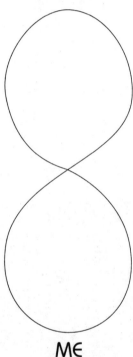

GOD
THE UNIVERSE

ME
THE EARTH

THE NUMBER EIGHT

The number 8 is a very important symbol for us to focus on in learning about this universal law. If the number 8 were turned on its side, it would represent the sign of infinity — no beginning and no end, eternity, God.

As we stand the infinity sign on end, it becomes the number 8. The top circle represents God, the universe, All That Is. The bottom circle represents the living creations of God –including Earth and us. As we look at the symbol of the number 8, it is obvious to us that the two circles are ever connected, flowing, one balancing the other.

There is but one God. God is spirit, existing in all things as energy, as love — unconditional love. God is within each of us, ready and willing to help us and to guide us to our highest good. God heals us and helps us prosper by fulfilling all our needs spiritually, emotionally, mentally and physically. As seen in the representation of the number 8 symbol, God is in each of us and each of us is in God — we are one energy.

We can experience this oneness with God through meditation. In meditation we go directly to God, to all wisdom, knowledge, love and truth, bypassing the outside world of other people's ideas, thought forms, confusion and negativity. It is said that God is all-seeing, all-powerful, that God is everywhere. Thus if we are one with God, that indicates to us that we too have these capabilities.

Expansion Meditation

Meditation is a quiet time where we can experience God in a way that is different from prayer. Meditation is a time when God speaks to us through our inner knowing. When we pray, we actually talk to God.

If there is a group of people, sit in a circle for this meditation. You can do this meditation alone if you choose.

Close your eyes. Breathe and relax the body with each breath. Focus on the center of your body, in the area between your solar plexus and heart. Feel a warm golden glow, and let that golden light expand until it fills your heart and every part of your body.

Extend the light outward even more, until it expands into the circle, the room, the outside world and beyond. Extend the light out into the universe until all you feel, all you see, all you know, is God. Feel the oneness, the peace, the love, the goodness that is part of you. Sit quietly for a moment until you feel at peace. Then, when you feel ready, take a deep breath and let your eyes open, coming back into the present moment.

When we are fully aware of the God within and practice this focus in all that we do, say, think and feel, we are in harmony with God's goodness and less involved with the physical world of negative thought forms.

God created us in His/Her image, perfect in all ways. Each of us has within our soul a special message system, a special coding that begins to expand our awareness as we grow spiritually, connecting us more strongly to our true relationship with God. This special coding reminds us that we have certain God-given gifts that are available to us through God's love for us.

Along with the gift of a physical body and the opportunity to experience Earth, we have been given free will, free choice. We can follow God's laws and create a wonderful, joyful life for ourselves, or we can operate from our conscious mind, using only our five physical senses, thus allowing ourselves to be influenced by our physical world. The physical world is full of negative thought forms and belief systems that can separate us from God and create in us fear, worry, stress and disease. We tend to follow our five physical senses because they are more real, more valid to us than the energy of God. We might feel that God does not exist in everyday reality because we can't sense God through using our physical senses of sight, hearing, touch, taste or smell.

It is important for us to know that God is real if we are, in fact, going to understand and use the Law of As Above, So Below. After all, how can we create Heaven on Earth if we truly do not believe God is real?

God makes Him/Herself a part of our life experience in many ways:

- In meditation, we go within ourselves. We turn off the sounds and thoughts of the outside world. We can ask questions of God while we are meditating and receive answers through our other senses of knowing, hearing thoughts (sometimes actual words), feeling or inner vision.

- God often speaks to us in the form of **symbols in our dream states and in small events** in our lives. For example, we might be having difficulty in making a very important change. We lose a key. The loss of the key is symbolic of a door closing behind us, one that we can no longer open because we do not have the key. We can struggle to open the door by other means, or we can simply acknowledge to ourselves that it is time to move on. Which way will work out more easily?

- God speaks to us by sending **special messengers** into our lives, people who come to teach and share with us certain spiritual principles that can help us make decisions about ourselves and where we are going, or people who act as mirrors, reflecting to us certain qualities of our own that we need to work on. As we see our lessons through these other individuals, it is easier to know what we need to work on within ourselves.

- God speaks to us through **certain books** we are led to read and through certain symbols that appear to us and through our everyday experiences. We might feel stuck, unable to move through a lesson. We are quietly encouraged to visit a bookstore and are guided to a specific shelf, even to a particular book. As we open the book we find our eyes moving to the very paragraph we need to read. There is our answer.

Can you think of other ways God speaks to us?

When we look at the number 8, we can see two circles joined together. One circle can represent what is real and the other circle can represent a mirror. When we think of the Law of As

GOD

Above, So Below, we become more aware that God is reflecting love and light down to us here on Earth so that we can become more and more aware of His/Her goodness and begin applying that goodness in our daily lives. We want to reflect God-like qualities in all that we do.

We are mirrors for each other. We draw to ourselves those people who can best reflect to us what we need to learn. If we need to be more loving and giving to others, we might draw to ourselves a very selfish friend to teach us what it feels like to be around someone who is selfish. Each type of person in our life reflects something

ME

we need to learn.

In the following chart make a special note of the types of people you feel you are drawing into your life. In the second column write in the lesson you feel you are to learn from the experience.

Type of person in your life

Lesson you feel you are learning

_____   _____

_____   _____

_____   _____

Now take a look at yourself in front of the mirror, a good look. Don't think anything, just look at yourself. What special qualities do you see in yourself that are qualities that God represents? For example, do you see a loving person, one who is happy and joyful? Make a note of all those qualities you see in yourself that you feel are the qualities that represent God. List those qualities you feel you need to work on to change.

Each of us is made up of four bodies: the physical, emotional, mental and spiritual. The physical body experiences life on Earth through the five senses of seeing, hearing, feeling tasting and smelling. The physical body is dense. When we are not in balance with God's universal laws, the physical body reacts through illness, disease or pain. Such problems in the physical body begin in the mental body as a thought long before they show up physically. Thus when we are not feeling whole and balanced in the physical body, we need to examine our thoughts and feelings to find out why.

The emotional body contains our feelings and emotions. Whether we are angry, happy, sad, ashamed, joyful and so on, the energy shows up in our emotional body as a specific color or vibration. When we read auras, we are reading the energy in the emotional body. The colors or energy tell us how the other individual is feeling. Pain and discomfort in the physical body is often seen as dark red, gray or black.

The mental body reflects our thoughts. When we are feeling good, we reflect happy thoughts. Through happy thoughts we create a happy environment in which to learn and grow. Often when we are small children, we hear things or feel things that lead us to believe we are not wanted, that we are not what our parent(s) expected, that we are not good enough, that we are not approved of. These thoughts create negative energy within ourselves that eventually leads to various forms of illness, including cancer. Thus it is important to always think positively about ourselves, no matter what we hear from others or what others would like us to believe about ourselves.

The spiritual body reflects God. It is a perfect, loving, positive energy. The more we reflect on this body, of working from this loving space, the happier we are.

As we work with this Law of As Above, So Below, we help create Heaven on Earth in all things for the benefit of everyone and everything. It is important to begin with ourselves, for all changes begins within each of us individually. Imagine within yourself how Heaven feels. Imagine that energy here on Earth. Create goodness through your thoughts, emotions and actions.

AFFIRMATION: I am open to God's truth, wisdom, knowledge, understanding, strength, power, love and goodness. God is a part of all that I do, think, feel and speak. Through God's love and guidance I create a happy, joyful life experience. My happiness is reflected out to others. What is created here on Earth is what God has created in Heaven and on Earth from the beginning.

4 • THE LAW OF POLARITY

When you ride a teeter-totter with a friend, you sit on a long board opposite from your friend. The board is centered over a pivot point, or fulcrum, a bar that holds the board in place and allows the ends to move up and down in a state of balance. To be balanced (when it is empty), the exact center of the board must rest on the bar so that both ends are in the air. If one side of the board is shorter or longer than the other, one end will touch the ground and not be balanced.

If you and your friend are about the same weight, you can take turns pushing the board up and down, working together to maintain balance. You can have hours of fun. As you move the board up and down, up and down, all is in balance and the ride is smooth and rhythmic.

What happens if your friend jumps or falls off the board? The balance is then disrupted. Your body weight can drive the teeter-totter hard into the ground, with you on it. You can try to use a teeter-totter by yourself, but you can move the board only as high as your legs are long. All you can do is jump up and down with the board between your knees. An imbalance exists because energy is not flowing evenly between the two ends of the teeter board.

God created the Law of Polarity, which states: Energy must flow evenly between two opposite points in order to achieve balance. Since all of creation was designed around the Laws of Balance and Harmony, the Law of Polarity is a vital part of creation, for without this law, balance and harmony cannot exist.

The Earth was created with opposites, or polarities. The North and South Poles are the ends of the axis that the Earth rotates around, in balance. North is at the "top" of the Earth (as we choose to view her), and south is at the "bottom." Thus we have become aware of two more polarities, or opposites — top and bottom. Can you think of others?

In examining the polarities of top and bottom, we can best understand the importance of balance through the following example:

In looking at a can of food, we see a metal cylinder that forms the can in which the food is contained. The top and bottom lids of the can seal the food inside the cylinder. If either the top or bottom were missing, the food could not stay in the can and could not flow between the two lids. Whenever energy does not flow freely back and forth between two points, it is not balanced.

By careful planning, God designed the Law of Polarity to maintain balance and harmony in the universe. To create balance, it is necessary for energy to flow freely and smoothly between two opposite points. If one of the two points is not present, the energy is out of balance, as we demonstrated in the examples of the teeter-totter and the can of food.

Thus as day was created, night was created also. God created the polarities of the Sun and Moon, summer and winter, spring and fall, right and left, male and female, up and down, the sky and the Earth and so forth. Each of these energies "opposed" another energy. A polarity exists between each of the pairs, for without the one, a balance in the energy that the polarities represent would not exist.

In examining the polarity of day and night, we find that the time between these two polarities offers us a space in which to work, play and sleep or rest. If only daytime existed, we would not perhaps be able to sleep. If there was only night, we might not want to go to work. Sunlight fills us with energy and vitality, the desire to exercise and move about. Moonlight and the dark of night calm us and bring us peace and the desire to sleep and rest.

God created polarities in the life experiences of all living things. A plant, for example, begins its life as a tiny seed and makes its transition from life to rebirth as the plant withers, dies (in the physical sense) and returns to the soil, leaving its seeds to grow into new plants. Just as the plant makes its transition, we do also, for we do not, in reality, "die." We merely move from a physical form back to a spiritual energy form, only to be reborn into a new physical body at the time we choose. A polarity exists between the time of birth and the time of passing. The energy that flows between these two polarities is that of learning and growing in the Earth school.

THE POLARITY OF MALE AND FEMALE

As souls, we have been born from the loving energy of God. Within each of us as souls exists the polarity of male and female energies. The male energy is seen as being strong, courageous, protective, outgoing; the female energy is felt to be soft, gentle, loving, nurturing.

To live on the Earth, we take the physical form that we feel will best help us learn the lessons we want to experience. We would look a bit silly if we were physically half man and half woman. Because our soul is both male and female energy combined, we have both male and female qualities within us. To be in balance within ourselves, we must balance the male and female polarities.

If we are too "male," we might appear to others to be too strong, aggressive or controlling. Or if we are too "female," we might be too soft and not stand up for ourselves. As we find the center of these two polarities of energy, we can stand in our own power in a loving way — loving but firm.

To bring the male and female energies within us into balance, the following exercise will be helpful.

Exercise

Sit in a quiet place where you will not be disturbed. Breathe very deeply, allowing each part of your body to relax more with each breath.

Focus your attention on your Heart Chakra. Feel the love in your heart. As you focus there, imagine that you are bringing the energy from your right side (the male side) into your heart. As you focus on your heart, imagine that you are bringing your female energy into your heart from your left side. See the two energies come together in your heart and feel the love.

Focus on your Solar Plexus Chakra just above the navel. Imagine a beautiful, bright golden yellow spot. Feel it grow larger and larger, brighter and brighter. Imagine now that you are pulling in your power from everyone and everything you feel you have given your power to by not following your heart, by doing what other people want you to do that you do not feel is right, by listening to other people rather than what is felt or heard from within yourself. Whenever we do not follow what we know is right for us, we give a little more of our power away.

As you stand in your power, see yourself and feel yourself and know yourself as balanced and centered. Feel all your energy in the center of your body as only one energy. No longer do you feel male energy or female energy, just loving God-energy. In this place the energy can flow back and forth between the right male side and the left female side without being too strong or too soft. This is the place where your body is in balance and harmony.

When we came to learn in the Earth school, God gave us a very special gift — free will, free choice. God intended that each of us use our free will in combination with our God-given powers and abilities to master the dense physical world. We came here to learn to maintain balance and harmony within ourselves, to assist in maintaining balance on the Earth, to operate from a place of love in our hearts, to know we are perfect in every way and to see that divine perfection in all of creation. We came here to learn about form and matter, about the power to create with our thoughts, and through love to maintain balance in all of creation. To succeed in this plan, we were to always maintain a strong bond to each other as souls and to God as one family of light.

We became more and more fascinated with the material world. Once we were in a physical body, we began to lose contact with God more and more. We felt we had to work hard to earn everything we wanted and needed. We began to believe in lack, disease, pain and suffering. We examined our connection to God and determined that perhaps we were not really part of God, or that God did not really exist. We decided to make the best of this world, to get whatever we needed however we could. We moved from a place of unity and oneness (we-us) to a place of separateness (you-me). As this change took place, we became aware of another polarity: oneness/separateness. Our goal was to find a balance between these two points.

THE POLARITY OF DARK AND LIGHT

From a Great Void, or empty space, God created the universe from love and light. At the time of creation, darkness merely represented the absence of light and love. From the energy of light/love came the universe created through the Law of Polarity to contain both light and dark in a positive way.

The opposites of dark and light were created to work together as a balancing force in the universe. Light was to represent daytime, activity, movement; dark was to represent nighttime, rest and relaxation. Mankind took this principle and twisted it a bit out of context as God designed it. Mankind saw darkness as the unknown, evil, bad; and light as goodness, the known. Mankind began to see him/herself as having both light and dark qualities. From this concept a whole new array of polarities or opposite energies were created.

The Native Americans refer to the dark part of us as the "shadow side" wherein lie our fears, concerns, anger, sadness, grief and the like. The shadow side is said to be a product of the Fall of Man, or that time when mankind began to pay more attention to material things than its spiritual growth. The me-self became more important than the God-self.

The following opposites were created:

THE LIGHT	THE SHADOW/DARK
Joy/Happiness	Sadness/Grief
Faith	Fear
Love	Anger/Hate
Peace	War/Conflict
Clarity	Confusion
Change	Limbo
Balance	Imbalance
Harmony	Disharmony
Health/Perfection	Disease
Life	Death
Trust	Deceit
Knowingness	Doubt
Oneness	Separateness
Goodness	Evil/Bad
Abundance	Lack
Freedom	Confinement
Trust	Distrust

Can you think of others? Make a list.

Instead of working from God-selves of love, happiness, joy, peace, health and abundance, humans began to operate from a place of separateness, fear, anger, sorrow, disease and lack. As each person became more and more focused on the human self, the many parts of God's creation became more and more affected by the imbalance.

If we are to fully express our God-selves and grow in God's light as was intended from the time we first came to Earth, we must not allow the shadow side of ourselves to control our experiences. To balance the polarities of dark and light within ourselves, we must become fully aware of those energies that are not of God, and through this awareness bring them into balance with the love in our heart, with the love that we are. As we come into balance, we come into a greater alignment with God and thus effect positive changes in all of creation. Through this balance we begin to heal much of the disharmony we created through our separation from God.

Exercise

Sit in a quiet place and take a few deep breaths, allowing the body to relax more and more with each breath. Take your attention to your heart and imagine a crystal clear-flame of light there. Feel the love in your heart. Imagine a flame contained within a tube that runs down the center of your body. Within the tube imagine two spirals of crystal-clear liquid light, one moving clockwise and the other moving counterclockwise.

Imagine the spirals of light moving up and down and in and out at will. Move the spirals up higher and higher until you feel the energy of God all around you, through your body and in your heart. Feel that love. Feel the peace and joy in that place.

Take your attention back into your heart and ask to examine those parts of your shadow side that need attention. Ask your fears, anger, resentment, guilt, shame, doubts and so on, to come into your awareness one by one. As you see what is there, send love to the energy, love to any person involved, and love to yourself. Forgive the person or situation. Forgive yourself for holding on to this energy. Examine the lesson you have learned from the experience and then release the energy into the spiral. See the energy transmuted or changed into love and light. Feel the freedom and balance within your body.

In working with the Law of Polarity, it is important to remember to maintain balance within yourself at all times. To maintain balance, you must find that place of centeredness within yourself where you do not have too much or too little energy given to one particular area of your life.

For example, you work very hard in school, studying all the time in an effort to make straight A's on your report card. If you do not find the balance, the opposite point of work which is play, you may become very frustrated and unhappy. If you work hard all the time and never take time out to do what you enjoy doing, you can become ill, a signal from your body that it is time to rest.

If you spend part of your day studying and part of your day resting, relaxing, going for a walk or doing things you enjoy, you will create a balance within yourself where you will find perfect health, happiness and a positive attitude which will create good grades and lots of great friends.

THE POLARITY OF GOOD/BAD, HEAVEN/HELL

From the basic idea of light/dark, good/evil, we created a polarity labeled heaven/hell. Some religious teachings express to us that hell is a place of punishment for not obeying God's laws, a place where the soul remains forever. Forever is a long time. God is love, and God loves each of us equally. We are here on Earth to experience lessons that we choose to learn. We are given free will to choose how we learn those lessons. Why, if God allows us to come to Earth to learn lessons, would He/She punish us for making a choice? Since we are, in fact, a part of God, if God were to punish us He/She would be punishing Him/Herself. Why would

God do that?

Do you have any fear about God punishing you? If so, where do you feel that belief came from? Does the belief feel valid or real to you? Do you see the belief as something coming from other people who do not fully understand God's truth? If you have any fear about God punishing you, write down the fear on a piece of paper, examine the fear and see where it is coming from, why you are holding on to it. Do not give the fear any energy, just examine it.

Exercise

Close your eyes and take a few deep breaths to relax your body. Again, create the flame in your heart, the flame within a tube in the center of your body with two spirals of clear liquid light moving clockwise and counterclockwise in the center of the tube. Move the spirals up and down in the center of your body within the tube and in and out from the center of your body, expanding and contracting the energy.

Move your attention upward, focusing on your picture of Heaven. Let the thoughts of Heaven come into your mind. Feel the presence of God all around you and in every part of your body. What do you see or feel? Can you feel the power and love from God?

Now ask your mind to focus on the word "hell." How do you feel as you focus on this word? Do you feel God? Is hell a real place as you sense it now? Do you have any fear about hell? If so, where did that fear come from? What is the lesson here to teach you?

If there is any fear, thank it for coming into your awareness. Forgive yourself for holding on to the fear, then release the fear into the spirals. See the fear dissolved in love and light.

Focus your attention on God. How do you perceive God? Is God loving and kind? Does God feel loving and kind and forgiving? Or do you feel that God would punish you for things you feel you do not do to please Him/Her? How do you feel about God?

If there are any fears about God punishing you, thank them for coming into your awareness. Forgive yourself for feeling this way and release the energy into the spiral. Imagine the love of God all around you. Feel the love as a warm blanket.

We have related angels and the masters and God to Heaven, to the light. Heaven represents to us beauty, love, peace, happiness, joy, abundance, perfection, everlasting life. When we think of hell, the images of Satan, the devil, fire, darkness, pain and suffering come to mind. Heaven-hell polarity exists in our conscious mind as reality. In fact, this whole concept is merely an illusion we have created as part of our life experience. To balance these polarities of thought, we must come into our heart center to the energy of love. Love is the balance between dark and light.

Just as God sent the Christ energy to Earth to teach love and oneness with the Creator, to share with us that all is possible when we believe it to be so, He/She also sent another energy as the polarity of Christ. Lucifer represents the dark, the shadow side; Christ represents goodness, light. As we learn in the Earth school, our choice through free will has given each of us the opportunity, lifetime after lifetime, to experience goodness as well as darkness. Through this experience we have been able to feel which avenue we choose to take as souls.

If we enter a life experience choosing to move from the light, to live a life not based on God's laws. Lucifer is the polarity energy with which we will be connected in our lessons. As we choose the path away from the light, we involve ourselves in Lucifer's energies of pain, suffering, war, hate, anger, sadness, grief and death. These are lessons we can choose to experience at any time. These are lessons that separate us from God and from our own true God-identity within ourselves. We have the free will to choose such an experience. The only punishment will be the unhappiness we create for ourselves in making such a choice.

In choosing a life of service to others, sharing, expressing joy, love, happiness, abundance and perfection, we work with the Christ energy. In this experience we grow closer to God. Our own lives are happy and abundant, for what we give out will return to us many times over what we give.

As we experience various lifetimes of dealing with the positive as well as the negative energies, we learn how to balance these experiences in our center and work from a place within of divine love. If we move too far into the shadow-side experiences, we do not find love and joy in our life. The more we focus on the God within us, the shadow side balances out into a place where we can love all these dark energies freely. Darkness has no power over us unless we give it power through fear and involvement in negative thinking.

We come into a greater alignment with our God-selves as we balance the dark and light energies within us. To properly work with the Law of Polarity, we must always be aware of our negative emotions, thoughts and feelings and not let their energy get the best of us. We must bring these energies into our center, release them in the spiral of light and balance them with divine love.

THE POLARITY OF ILLUSION AND REALITY

In the free-will experiment, mankind has created many illusions upon the Earth. Illusions are things that seem real to us but in actuality are not real. One illusion is that God punishes us for doing wrong things. The reality is, there is no good or bad: there is only love. Good and bad are opposites within the Law of Polarity that we must balance within ourselves to grow as souls.

As we look around the Earth, we see trees, flowers, streams, animals, people, buildings. Everything appears real to our conscious minds. In other words, because we can see, hear, feel, taste and smell our world, everything appears to be very much a part of our experience. To humans in physical form, the physical world seems very real.

All is energy. We are energy. Energy is constantly changing, moving, growing. Energy vibrates at different speeds. The denser the energy, the slower the vibration. In our physical bodies, the Earth and all her living things seem very real to us because they are vibrating at the same slow speed as we are. In our energy bodies, however, we soon see the Earth and all of creation in a different light. We see creation as moving particles of energy, taking shape as they are directed by thought.

Everything is created from a thought. Whatever we think, we create. Just as quickly as we create something in our mind, we can change that thought to something else. As we think of something, that something begins to take form. Soon it is form. We have created a form from what we were thinking.

We create illusions from our thoughts. We believe that we cannot heal ourselves, that we cannot walk through walls. We look at the mass of our physical bodies and think: "There is no way I could possibly jump that high. I can't walk through walls." If we think it is impossible to accomplish something, it *is* impossible. We create a limitation with our minds. When we believe *all is possible*, we create a reality through this belief that we can do anything we set our minds to do.

One of the greatest illusions we have created on Earth is the illusion of disease. We were created in the divine image of God as perfect. We are perfect in every way. In this God-perfection there is no pain, suffering or disease.

As we label things, we give them thought energy. As we give thoughts energy, we create. We get a runny nose. We label the symptom a cold but we have created what we thought about, believed or feared. If we notice our runny nose and simply acknowledge, "I am perfect and balanced" and mean it, the runny nose will not become a cold. The runny nose might, be a cleansing of the sinuses. We could honor the runny nose as a part of clearing away old thoughts and feelings and let the perfection of our true God-being shine through. The illusion is the cold; the reality is perfection. In perfection there is only perfect health.

God, divine love, perfection and abundance are reality. All that is not of these qualities is illusion. That our soul light is one with God at all times is reality. To believe in death is illusion. Our soul never dies, for it is energy that has the ability to move from one form, the physical, to another form, pure light. As we begin to acknowledge our own divine light within us, as we begin to focus on the love that we are, we create balance between these polarity points. We are actually here on Earth to experience and master the lessons in working with the energies of illusion created here, while expanding the wisdom of our soul — true reality.

POLARITY AND THE EARTH

If we were to take a trip around the world to visit people in different countries, we would find some people with nice homes, automobiles, plenty of warm clothing and good food and who have a positive, happy attitude about their lives. On the other hand, we could also visit countries where people are very poor and have little or no food and clothing, no warm shelter and where they are feeling very unhappy and lonely. We could say about this that there is polarity in the world: the polarities of rich/poor, happy/sad, lack/abundance and so on.

This is not how God intended the Law of Polarity to be used. God gave mankind a beautiful garden in which to live, where all needs could be taken care of. Through misuse of free will, mankind created selfishness, and attempted to take power from others, to control other people and the Earth. Through this misuse mankind created imbalance and an unhealthy world where we are presently experiencing war, drought, famine, disease, unhappiness, confusion and chaos — as well as love, joy, peace and abundance. Each of us has free will to change this picture, to learn to stay in own power, to share the riches of this planet, to work together and live in harmony with each other and all of creation.

There will always be the polarity of day and night, the universe and the Earth, the Sun and Moon, man and woman. But mankind does not have to continue playing the game of good/bad. The imbalances we have created on the Earth must be corrected if we are to survive. Where do we begin the task of creating balance?

- **Me to we.** We must each release the great concern with the self and begin to take note of what is right for the Whole, for each of us together as souls sharing the Earth. It is time to plan for the future, work together. Living on the Earth is a team effort.
- **Honor the Earth and all of creation.** We must take from the Earth only what we need to live happy, healthy lives. To save our Earth, we must replace trees we cut down and learn to build our homes in a way that protects instead of depletes the environment. We must learn to work with natural products that nourish the Earth instead of destroying her natural resources.

At present we are experimenting with various ways in which we can harness the natural energy of the Earth — wind, water and sunlight. In this way, we are protecting the fossil fuels — coal, oil and natural gas deposits. As fossil fuels are removed from the Earth, huge holes are often left where they were extracted, holes that can cave in and cause further damage to the Earth's structure.

We should limit the use of concrete, allowing the Earth to breathe and renew herself, and protect the soil we use to grow the food that sustains us as living beings. Let's love our Earth. She can survive without us — but can we survive without the Earth's natural resources?

- **Learn to recycle.** By recycling we eliminate garbage sites containing tons of cast-off items. We can easily find ways to reuse many of our throwaways, such as glass, aluminum and paper products. We need only to care enough to do so, to take the time to recycle and protect the Earth.
- **Be responsible for ourselves.** It is important for us to take responsibility for ourselves, our own well-being, and learn how to follow our own inner guidance instead of the people around us. We must develop our leadership qualities, stand in our own power, become self-sufficient. We are not here to continue playing the same game as our ancestors. Structure as we know it is breaking down, because it is time for change. This change is important to our future and the future of the Earth.

- **Remember that we are all brothers and sisters.** In God's family, we are all one with each other. Thus we have no right to make judgments against others when they do things we do not like. Each of us is here to learn lessons. We must allow other people to learn their lessons and expect them to allow us to learn our lessons. See each person as a brother or sister in God's family no matter what they say, do or believe. Honor and love ourselves. Honor and love all others equally.
- **God is in all of creation.** Realize that God is in all things everywhere. Where there is God, there is love, perfection, goodness. Thus, if God is everywhere, love, perfection and goodness must be everywhere as well.

In appropriately applying the Law of Polarity in our daily lives, it is important to remember that all energy must flow equally between two opposites for there to be balance. We must become fully aware of who we are as parts of God. We have created a world of separateness, but the polarity of separateness is oneness and unity. As we meditate and find our center in the spirals of light, we can transmute the negative thoughts, feelings and emotions that separate us from God. As we do so, we come into a balance in our center.

While we live in a world that does not fully reflect the love it was created from, we do not have to experience or reflect the negative energies within ourselves. We do not have to feel sad, angry, lonely or ill. We have a choice. Whatever we choose to be and experience, we will create.

In all situations where opposites exist, the very center of the two polarities is balance. Thus, if we are feeling very, very angry, we can send just a small amount of love into the anger, and then more and more love until we are filled with love and the anger is transmuted. In this love we are free of negative feelings; in this love we find balance.

The Law of Polarity exists in every part of our life experiences. Whether we are lacing our shoes, adding just enough milk to our cereal, balancing the checkbook or keeping our thoughts on God and love, we are working with this important law. Without the Law of Polarity, balance and harmony would not exist. The universe as we know it to be would not exist.

AFFIRMATION: Each day I stay centered and balanced, allowing my energy through thoughts, feelings and emotions to move freely. I choose to focus on love, light and goodness. I surrender my free will to God's will, and through my surrender I am balanced and free.

5 • THE LAW OF CYCLES

The Law of Cycles can be observed on our Earth in the seasons of spring, summer, fall and winter; in the growth of plants from seed to the mature plant to its passing and the reseeding for new growth. We see the Law of Cycles in animals, insects, birds and in people as they move from their birth into maturity to the time for leaving the body and preparing for rebirth in a new body.

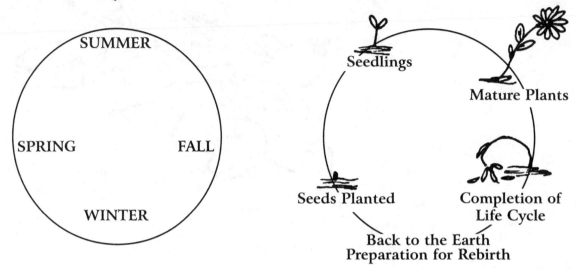

To help you understand this law, plant a seed and care for it lovingly. Watch it grow into a full-grown plant and then see it begin to decay and be reabsorbed back into the Earth. You will notice as the plant begins to die that it leaves behind seeds that you can plant to grow more new plants just like the one passing away. The plant that is passing away nourishes the soil with her body so the young seedlings will sprout and thrive.

Each of us comes to Earth to learn a particular lesson. In learning the lesson, our soul moves closer and closer to God's love and light. Perhaps you are here to learn to love all things without condition. This lesson may take you through various experiences where you are dealing with very different or uncaring people. God lovingly tests you along the way to point out to you whether or not you are learning the lesson. Each lesson can be learned easily and effortlessly if we work from the energy of our Higher Self, our God-self, rather than from the conscious ego of our physical bodies.

Learning a lesson about unconditional love may find us involved with a friend who calls us names or hurts us in some way. Our task is to send love to him/her and never let the other person's feelings affect how we choose to feel.

The Law of Cycles becomes more familiar to us through our lessons on Earth. If we pay close attention to certain experiences that are happening over and over again, the pattern shows us we have not yet learned the lesson.

Sometimes we do not want to make changes in our life, but to learn the lesson we must agree to make a change. It could mean that we need to move to a new city, meet new friends, change schools, or simply think and act in a different way. We may have been taught to believe a certain way about God and who God is when in fact we feel differently about the entire subject. If we follow our own feelings, the lesson moves on to something different. If we listen to others rather than ourselves, often we stay stuck in the same situation until we honor our feelings and make the appropriate changes.

What lessons can you think of that seem to be happening over and over again in your life at the present time? For example:

  •Do you have friend after friend who tries to push you around and make you do what they want, even when you choose not to?

  •Do you often hold back on saying things to people that you know are things they need to hear or fail to express your feelings, simply because you are afraid they will not want to to be around you any longer?

•Do you often find yourself making fun of others and having a difficult time making friends?

•Do you often look for someone else to follow, always feeling that other people are probably right, stronger than you or better able to lead than you?

•Do you hesitate to sign up for class officer, sports captain or an important position on the team and so on, simply because of a fear that you might not be chosen and thus feel like a failure?

•Do you feel other people have so much more than you do and thus feel embarrassed by your clothing, your home, car, belongings?

Make a list of those experiences taking place in your life that make you feel unhappy.
Are they happening over and over again?
What do you feel these experiences are trying to show you?
What haven't you learned?
What do you feel you need to do to learn the lesson?

Complete the following story based on what you have learned from the above information. Billy was very unhappy and lonely. He had few if any friends. He would lie on his bed and think about himself, wondering why everyone else in the whole world had friends except for him.

Billy did not like himself. He felt he was not friendly enough, not popular enough, not outgoing enough. "I know," he thought. "It's because I don't have a boat like Jackie. That's it. If I had a boat, Jackie would be my friend."

"But no, that couldn't be it because Jackie always invites Paul and Karen to go to the river with him and his family. Paul and Karen don't have a boat," Billy thought.

"I know what . . . Freddie would be my friend if I had a new racing bike like his dad bought him. That's it. Well . . . no . . . he and Suzie are friends, and she has an old beat-up bike that belonged to her mother. Hmmmmm."

Billy just couldn't figure out why he didn't have any friends. He thought and thought. What was this lesson all about?

Can you complete this story to help Billy see better why he doesn't have any friends? What can he do to make more friends?

What is Billy's lesson?

What things did Billy change that helped him to find new friends and to be happier?

Let's look at a cycle of your own life experience. Close your eyes and let your body relax. Imagine a relaxing energy moving into your feet and all through your body, helping you relax more and more.

Exercise

Let your mind go back to a time when you were born. You are a tiny baby and you came into this world with certain needs —a need for food, warmth and love. You are totally dependent on someone else's caring for you. You are helpless on your own. Yet at this time in your life, you are very close to the angels. The angels love and protect you and you feel happy and secure.

You begin to grow as a child, and as you grow you learn lessons from your parents, brothers and sisters, teachers and friends. You learn as you experience the world. You are still not able to take care of yourself, but you are learning to dress yourself, tie your shoes, brush your hair and teeth and feed yourself.

It is important to know that as we learn from others, we often begin to follow what others feel and believe rather than what we feel and believe inside. Each of us is important. We have certain things we feel very strongly about, and we need to act on these feelings to honor what we feel and to feel good in expressing these feelings to others.

If we live in a home filled with love and joy, we grow up to feel that love and joy are a natural part of us. If we grow up in a home of anger and abuse, we begin to feel angry and tend to abuse others as a bully or in other ways. Our thoughts, feelings and actions are reflections of our environment.

As we become young adults, we begin to enter the world of school and job situations. Now we hear what our teachers want us to hear and what our employers want us to know and do for them. We tend to listen and follow, accepting what is offered, with the idea that since these people are older than we are and have been out in the world longer than we have, they should know more about what is right than we do.

It is a lesson for us to honor our feelings. We know inside who we really are —a child of God. We are created from love to be love and to express love as well as receive love. We learn the importance of sharing with others and learning to work in harmony and balance with all living things.

As we reach maturity, we move through a cycle of change. We may marry and have children, change jobs several times or move to different cities to live. We meet people who become our friends and just as quickly these friends leave to make room for new friends to enter our life. Each new cycle of friends comes to us at a time when we are experiencing a new lesson and growing spiritually. The more we grow and act in a spiritual way and the more friends we allow into our lives who are loving and spiritual, the easier our lives begin to flow.

When we enter the cycle of old age we often feel that it is time to retire. It needs to be a time of retirement only if we choose it to be so. Now is the time when you can be free of obligations to others, responsibilities to family and friends, a time to begin to enjoy hobbies, a different career, going back to school, learning something new, traveling and meeting new people, volunteering time to share love with others. It does not have to be a time when you sit at home alone and wait to leave the Earth. It can to be a time of great joy and happiness.

You now leave your body. This life cycle is complete. You travel back to the world of spirit, back to the Source of all life. Here you meet other friends and relatives who have passed on before. Here you are given an opportunity to review the lesson you learned in this life, to decide for yourself if the lessons are complete or if it is necessary to return once more and experience again.

In your soul body you are pure energy, pure light. You can float up and down, back and forth. You can think of a place you want to be and then be there in an instant. You can see, hear, smell, taste, feel or sense things as you did in your body, but much more intensely. You are able to see and hear more clearly in your lightbody.

Although you no longer eat foods as you did on Earth, you still have the same sense of taste and smell, but are much more sensitive to the fragrant and beautiful world of spirit. Your feeling senses are greater. You are ultra-ultrasensitive — far more sensitive than when you were on Earth in a physical body. And once more you are one with God, energy with energy.

After a period of time you again choose to return to Earth. You can choose a male or a female body, depending on what you wish to learn. Sometimes it is easier to learn in a female body than a male and vice versa. For example, if you are here to learn to love someone equally, perhaps you will choose a female body in order to feel freer to express a nurturing type of love. Or perhaps you choose a male body to have a more challenging lesson to give love. You are the one who decides.

When you return to Earth, you return in the stage of birth. All the wonderful events and knowingness of the spirit world becomes veiled, so you lose touch somewhat with the love and joy you experienced while in your lightbody. As you reenter the Earth world into a new family, a new city and country, a new lesson, you begin again. Each time you come to the Earth school, you learn one more lesson that helps your soul and God better understand what it is like to have an emotional, mental and physical body.

In coming to Earth you have a physical body that sees, hears, feels, tastes and smells. It also has the ability to feel from a higher sense, through your intuition, a knowing that comes from your soul and from God. We often call intuition the voice within. It is your guidepost. Your challenge is to learn to listen and follow inner guidance while learning and experiencing the Earth school from your physical senses and conscious mind. The physical body has density, which is limited in what it can do. If you don't take care of it, it often becomes sick. The body ages because we believe we have to grow old, when in fact our body's cells all renew themselves every seven years. Thus we have a brand-new body every seven years. So take care of the body. It will serve you well much longer.

On Earth we also deal with the emotional body. In the world of spirit we express and experience universal love, joy, happiness, peace, health and prosperity. Here on Earth, through free will, mankind has created many negative emotions — anger, hate, greed, selfishness and so on. We are here to learn to balance this body and our emotions so that we can always operate from a place of love, joy, peace, happiness, wholeness and abundance.

The mental body houses our conscious mind as well as our subconscious or hidden thoughts. We have been given the gift of thought, and by thinking something, we create it. Our lesson is to think loving, positive thoughts and grow in our lessons in a positive, loving way.

The spiritual body, our Higher Self, is always connected to God and exists in both the spiritual and physical worlds. Our Higher Self does not have to express the negative thought forms of Earth. It remains ever connected to God and all goodness.

As we tune in more and more to our Higher Self and go about our daily chores from that perspective, we can better understand why we are here and how we can live on Earth without accepting the negative feelings and thoughts that exist here.

AFFIRMATION: I clearly see who I truly am, a child of God — of love, peace and joy. I am here to learn in the Earth school, to understand that life is a wonderful gift to cherish and that death is merely a return to God in preparation for my rebirth. I am open to change and transition, because change and transition are good. Through change and transition I grow closer to God.

6 • THE LAW OF CAUSE AND EFFECT

There is but one mind in all the universe, the mind of God. Think of God as being the center of a large wheel. Each of us is a spoke of this wheel, extending outward, but ever connected to God.

God, the center of the wheel, sees all, knows all and is all truth. God is all goodness. In this God-mind there is no judgment, no negative thought forms, no punishment — only love, joy, happiness, peace, abundance, health and perfection.

Think of your connectedness to this center. You are a spoke of the wheel. The thought forms, the God-energy, can flow from God to you and back to God, an unending flow of energy. Through the mind of God and our connectedness to it, we have the ability to create our own reflection or image of God's positive, loving thoughts in our own life experiences on Earth. God's thoughts are projected down the spokes to each of us equally, without judgment, without discrimination. What happens to this energy? From this beautiful God-goodness energy we create negative thought forms about ourselves, our family, our friends, school, teachers, society and the world. How is this possible? In your opinion, what takes place within our own consciousness to change God's positive, loving thought to some of the thought forms we find on Earth?

Each of us was given the gift of free will in our Earth experience. Through the misuse of this special gift, mankind has moved further and further in thoughts, actions and deeds from the God-mind. What are some of your own thoughts you feel are creating a break in the flow of thought from God to you?

"In the beginning was the word and the word was God." And "God is love." Because we were created in the image of God, we were created in love. Thus any thought, word or action that is not coming from that love within each of us is creating an imbalance, disharmony, discord within our own lives as well as within our environment and the world. We can think of our life experiences as reflections from a giant mirror. We each have a pure connection to God's mind, which can be reflected back to each of us on Earth and utilized in our life experiences. However, we sometimes allow our conscious mind to interfere and block the smooth flow of thought between God and ourselves.

You are a very powerful person here on Earth. In every thought you think, in every word you speak, you are creating your life experiences and creating the world around you. Look at your own life. You will see that there is rarely any moment when you are not thinking a thought or expressing yourself verbally. Here lies your power. Every thought and word you think and speak, whether positive or negative, creates your life experiences.

What we think, we create. What we think about ourselves becomes our reality. Every thought we are thinking right at this very moment is creating our future. What are you thinking right now? Is it positive or negative?

Exercise

For this exercise you will need a large magnet and nails, screws, tacks and paper clips.

Try different ways to use the magnet to draw different objects to it. Consider your thoughts to be the attracting power of the magnet and the objects all the experiences you draw to yourself everyday. You can see just how your negative thoughts can be detrimental to the soul's evolution.

Whatever we think about or focus on most of the time is stored in our energy field, our aura. The aura vibrates as pure energy. It sends impulses in the form of electrical current into the universe. Like this magnet, these thoughts bring into our lives just what we have been thinking and believing as our truth. Whether positive or negative, we attract people and situations into our lives to help us recognize which thoughts and words we need to correct in order to restore balance with God's love.

Through our ability to recognize which areas of our thinking and speaking processes are not coming from a God-space, we are able to change those patterns through positive thinking and speaking and through creating affirmations of positive thought patterns, thus changing our own life experiences and situations in the world around us.

Meditation

Let's look carefully at ourselves to determine how our thoughts and words may be affecting us, how we see ourselves and others, how we relate to our families and friends and other people around us, and how we view our school experiences, our community and the world.

Sit in a comfortable position, spine straight. Take a few deep breaths, relaxing your body more and more with each breath. Allow your conscious mind to flow into a peaceful connection to that place within yourself where you connect with God. Feel the strength, the power, the love, joy and happiness that comes to you as you connect with God.

Imagine you are standing in front of a large mirror. The mirror is reflecting back to you images regarding different aspects of your life experiences here on Earth. Pay close attention to how you might create a more perfect life experience for yourself and a more perfect world by changing your thought processes in the different areas of your life that we will explore in this meditation.

First, look at your body. Begin with the top of your head and slowly let your eyes move downward, examining every aspect of yourself. How do you feel about your body? Are you happy with what you see? Do you have any thoughts about yourself that might to be creating disharmony in your life? Is your hair the wrong color, your nose too large or too small? Are you too fat, too thin? Are you too tall or too short?

Now visualize yourself as perfect in every way, a reflection of God. "I am a beautiful, happy, loving reflection of God. I am perfect in every way. I love myself and accept myself just as I am."

Your family members now are reflected in the mirror. How do you see your relationship to your mother, father, brothers and sisters? Do you feel loved, accepted, respected? Or do you feel left out, rejected, different? Are you able to communicate openly with your family members, or do you feel they will never understand you? Do you feel that one family member is loved more than you or given more attention than you, or is everyone treated equally?

Imagine having the perfect family relationship, like one large circle, where each gives and receives from the other equally. Feel the love flowing in your family unit. See your family as you would like them to be. "I give and receive equally in my family unit. We are happy, joyful and loving. God is the center of our family unit and brings to us joy and peace."

Visualize your friends. Do your friends treat you as you would like to to be treated? Do you have friends who are happy? Do you have friends who are angry? Are you angry? Do your friends include you in their activities or do you feel left out?

Now create beautiful, loving friendships. See all your friends happy and joyful, sharing their experiences with you. Remember, the more love you feel within yourself and the more love you express outward and the happier, more joyful your thoughts and conversations, the more loving and joyful friendships you will bring to yourself. "I experience loving and joyful relationships with my friends. I am accepted and I accept them, just as we are, perfect in every way."

How do you see your school experience? Do you see school as a burden, a place where you are forced to participate and wish you did not have to attend? Or is school a wonderful place to connect with others and participate in a learning and growing situation? Do you enjoy your studies, or do you find them a burden?

See school as a place of learning and growing. Everything comes to you easily and effortlessly – good grades, time to study, friendships, great teachers.

Imagine school as a place of sharing and exchanging ideas and experiences with new friends. See school as a bridge in the process of maturing and venturing out into the world as a whole, complete, prepared being. "I do well in school. School is a wonderful place of learning and growing. I have plenty of time to study and make good grades."

As you view your community, how do you feel? Are there things within your community that you would like to change? Are there not enough places for young people to go to have a good time?

Are there parts of your community where people are suffering and you would like to see some changes made? Are there certain rules and regulations you have experienced that seem unfair?

Visualize your community as perfect, where everyone shares and cares about one another. See the community just as you would like it to to be, with you as a caring participant. Feel the happiness, the joy, the love within your community. "I create a loving and joyful environment, because I am loving and joyful within myself. I express this love and joy in all that I do, think and say."

Now take a good look at the world around you. What do you see? What are some of the things that make you unhappy? What are some of the things you are happy with? What would you like to change? Do you see poverty, illness, crime and angry, fearful people? Do you see happy, joyful, loving people who always express God in all that they do? How can you change what you do not like?

Change begins with you. Radiate from your heart all the God-love that you can be. Send this love out into the world. Imagine that as this God-love touches all the parts of the Earth that need healing, the love changes everything negative to everything loving and positive. Now imagine the world just as you would like to see it. "All is perfect in my world. All is divine love."

Focus your attention on what you have just created within yourself and outside of yourself, in your family, school, community and the world. See your environment just as you want it to to be. Focus all the love you can on this image. Open your eyes when you feel ready to do so.

How did you feel about the changes you made in this meditation? Do you feel that if you keep envisioning them, they will change? Why? Why not?

THE LESSON OF KARMA

How many times has a friend made you feel hurt or angry? In such a situation if you became very angry, your friend might also have become more and more angry until perhaps you began to hit each other.

In this situation angry energy begins to grow. The anger from each of you grows more and more intense until you feel that all you can do is strike your friend. As you lash out, you create an action that requires a reaction for balance. This reaction is your friend striking you back.

Everything is energy. Energy is all around and within us, and it is involved in our breathing, walking, running, eating, drinking, playing — in all that we do and think. Because thoughts are energy, whatever we think is sent out to someone else and to the universe. If it is a negative thought, we can expect a negative thought or action to come back to us.

Whatever you send out you receive back, not out of punishment, but simply as a lesson demonstrating the Law of Cause of Effect. This law teaches us to to be careful about what we think — to think positive, loving thoughts.

Let's look at a situation where in one lifetime a man steals a car. He drives the car, knowing he did not pay for it; the car does not belong to him. Yet he does not return the car. He might go through this whole life experience stealing and thinking he will never get caught. Perhaps he never gets caught . . . or perhaps he does and spends the rest of his life in prison, very unhappy.

By stealing the car, this man is creating what is called a karmic debt. He owes the people he stole from, but not necessarily in the form of money. Perhaps this man comes back to Earth as a very poor man or woman, having nothing. No one will help him. He struggles and struggles. He finds some food and a pair of shoes in a garbage dump. He tucks his prizes under his arm, then sets them down for a moment only to be stolen by another individual. He may spend his entire lifetime homeless and penniless.

This is just one example of a possible karmic lesson that could be created. The lesson comes from breaking the laws of God. In the Ten Commandments God has told us, "Thou shalt not steal," meaning that it is not right to take away what another has.

Now, let's say this same man stole the car and then returned it to the individual he stole it from, paying him for its use. Even though it was not right to steal the car, he came back to make right what he had done that was out of harmony with the other man's experience. The other man's lesson was perhaps to forgive and accept the payment and apology.

The first individual might be learning that stealing from others brings feelings of guilt and that stealing is inappropriate behavior because it hurts the person experiencing the loss. The other individual may be learning to allow a certain experience in his/her life, and to accept apology and restitution without accusation, blame or anger. In this situation all karma can be completed and no further experience need take place for either individual because the lesson has been learned.

Let's look at some ways we can create karmic cause and effect in our lives.

THE CAUSE (ACTION)	THE EFFECT (REACTION)
You tell a lie.	You are punished when truth is discovered. You feel guilty, ashamed and very unhappy.
You cheat on a test.	The teacher finds out. Although you could have received a better grade on the test, because you were caught cheating the teacher gave you an F. Your parents ground you and you're forced to sit at home while your friends are out playing and having fun.
You share your lunch with a friend who forgot hers.	Your friend brings you a gift and buys you a great lunch the next day.
You make fun of a child of a different color.	You travel to another country. You are the minority. All eyes are on you. People are staring, pointing fingers and laughing at you.
You label another child "retard" because you think he is not as smart as you. She asked you to help her study for a biology test. You said, "No way." You are afraid your friends will abandon you if you are friends with her.	She receives an A on the math test and you get a C. You discover she excels in the subjects you do not. She is willing to tutor you in math in exchange for your tutoring her in biology. You discover she is really a great friend.
You decide people who are poor are not as good as you and are actually dangerous.	Your car breaks down on a lonely road. A poor farmer and his family drive you into town to offer you a place to stay while your car is being repaired. You learn about shar-

Can you list some other ideas and feelings about the energy of cause and effect? What lessons do you think you are learning from your list?

Remember . . .

If you:	*You create:*
think anger	more anger
judge others	you are judged
steal from another	you lose
cause another pain	you receive pain in return
help another unselfishly	receive something more in return
love all beings equally	receive more love, happiness and joy

AFFIRMATION: *Thoughts are positive, powerful tools which I am now using to create my life as loving, joyful, peaceful and abundant. I fill myself with divine love as my thoughts are filled with God. Through these thoughts the peace, love and light that I am reaches out into my family, friends, school, community, the Earth, and touches everyone I meet. God and I are one.*

7 • THE LAW
OF DIVINE LOVE

God has always been, is now, and always will be a source of great love, power and wisdom. We often hear God described in various sources of literature as being *omnipresent* (God is everywhere in all things, at the same time, all the time); *omnipotent* (God is all-powerful; there is no being or thing more powerful than God); and *omniscient* (God is all-seeing, all-knowing; seeing and knowing everything everywhere in the universe).

There is another term we can use to describe God. God is all-love, all the time, for everything, everyone, everywhere. God is complete within Him/Herself as a force of power in divine love. God's love is constant, flowing in and out, equal, nonjudgmental, unconditional, unlimiting, healing and balancing.

When God created the universe, the Earth, mankind and all living things, God infused a part of Him/Herself in all that was created. This part of God is termed the "divine blueprint" and exists at the cellular level in the structure of all living things. This divine blueprint, this part of God which was infused in all things at the time of creation, is divine love. Divine love can be said to be the "glue" that holds all things in the universe together. Without this glue, this love, we would not exist as we are. None of God's creation would exist as we know it.

Divine love is *unconditional love,* or love without conditions. This means that divine love is a part of all living things without exception. Divine love is at the very center of the life experience of all living things no matter where they live, what they believe, how they think and act or how they look.

Unconditional love is love in the purest form, and it works to create balance and harmony in all living things, in all life experiences, in the entire universe, all of the time. Love in this state has no conditions, no bonds, no restrictions or limitations, no requirements or expectations, no judgment, no barriers. Because this form of love is so pure, it does not create pain, sorrow, lack, disease, disharmony or imperfection. It creates no separation between God and all living things.

God expresses unconditional love in the rainbow that follows a storm and brings to each of us a sense of peace and joy; in a smile or hug that makes us feel happy and loved; in a flower that brightens our day; in a bird that sings a beautiful melody; in a stream that brings serenity and peace to our bodies, minds and souls. God's love is expressed in all things.

God's love can brighten the darkest moment, calm the most angry person, heal the impossible, prevent a war or conflict, connect people from all walks of life and all beliefs. God's love is pure and simple:

"I love you equally, all the time, every moment of every day. I have loved you since the beginning of time and will love you to eternity, which is forever. No matter what you feel you have done that is not loving and kind, I LOVE YOU. There is nothing I will not give to you or do for you. I will never punish you, for you are part of me. Why would I punish myself? You are here to learn lessons, to experience the physical world. I have given you free will on the Earth, allowing you free choices in your life experience either to follow a spiritual path and maintain balance and harmony according to My universal laws, or to choose a path not in balance with My laws.

"There is nothing you cannot heal within yourself, for you were created from Me and are already perfect. It is only the illusions of the Earth that create for you a feeling of imperfection. Only the thoughts from the Earth consciousness can cause you to feel separate from Me for we are forever one. The love that I am exists in your heart. Only when you do not allow yourself to experience My love do you feel alone, hurt, angry or sad.

"When you focus your thoughts on Me and My loving presence, you are happy, joyful, loving, compassionate, at peace, healthy and abundant. These qualities exist in the state of balance and harmony that I have created in all things. Any thought, feeling or emotion that does not represent one or more of these qualities of goodness, has been created within your own conscious mind from what you have experienced in the Earth school in the past or present, what you hear from other people, what you accept from the world as truth. Fears, doubts, concerns and worries, pain and suffering are all from the conscious thought forms that surround you when you are not in balance and harmony with all of creation. Think love. Be love, be happy! I love you! I AM."

When we think, act and feel from a place of unconditional love within our hearts, we see the divine aspect of every living thing God has created. We see God through love as a part of all creation, and God within us. In this beautiful place within our hearts we are centered, balanced, at peace with ourselves and the world. We feel and express joy in all that we do. Good things happen in our life experiences. We feel we have value, that we are special. We develop a sense of unity with each other, regardless of any physical differences or spiritual beliefs. The *you-me* concept merges into the greater whole, becoming the *we* of balance and harmony. We focus on what is good for the whole, for all of us together as one family. We are concerned for everyone in the world equally, and for the Earth herself. We release the feelings of selfishness and greed, what's good for *me*, what I want only for myself.

Love is a beautiful gift that we all share equally. No one can take that love from us. Love is in every cell of our being and flows in and out, giving to others and receiving for ourselves. Love does not bring pain, only joy. Love of the highest order, divine love, is what each of us has come to share with all of creation, with each other. Through divine love we each find peace and freedom.

Through experimenting with the lessons to be learned from free will, mankind has distorted the true meaning of the energy of love, as God intended love to be defined. Mankind created its own kind of love in the physical world — as a feeling expressed between man and woman, parent and child, brother and sister, between family members and special friends. In many ways this physical love became a way of controlling and manipulating others. Physical love was designed as love with conditions, judgment and limitation. The statements "I will love you if you buy me that bicycle" and "I will love you more if you get good grades in school" demonstrate that love will be given only if something is done first to satisfy the desire of the person offering the love. Mankind's physical love states, "I will love you if . . ."; God's divine love offers, "I love you unconditionally, without expectation, judgment or limitation."

Physical love is not always a positive experience. There are times when people express only physical, conditional love, forgetting all about God's love within themselves. There are those who say to each other in one moment, "I love you," and in the next moment are fighting, separating, going in different directions. In situations such as this, people expressing conditional love are only concerned with themselves and their personal needs. If the other person does not meet those needs or demands, the other individ-  ual quickly assumes they are not loved or appreciated. Jealousy, envy, lack of support, guilt, shame, competition, greed, self-centeredness and the like can often consume a relationship between two people that began as physical love.

DIVINE LOVE IS THE MOST POWERFUL VIBRATION IN THE UNIVERSE. Divine love knows no negative energy, no negative thoughts, feelings or actions. *Can't, don't, shouldn't, bad* and so on are words that do not exist in the expression of love. Divine love is all-powerful because God is all-powerful and God is love. This love exists in all of creation, regardless of actions and beliefs. Even when there is war, conflict, illness, disharmony, pain, suffering, love is still present. Love is the basic structure of who we all truly are — a part of God. Thus no matter how we feel or behave, no matter what we feel we have done wrong, the love of God is ever present within us. We are never separate from God; thus we are never separate from divine love.

It is important to note that there is no problem we can ever face in the Earth school that enough love will not solve, no loneliness that enough love will not erase. There is no disease that enough love will not heal, no darkness that enough love will not illuminate. There is no situation that enough love cannot change, no differences that enough love will not correct. By living, breathing and expressing divine love, we each have the power to maintain within ourselves perfect health, happiness, peace, joy and abundance. Through love we can forgive and release anything within us that no longer serves us. By changing ourselves, by expressing more and more love within ourselves and outwardly, by our example we help change others. When we apply the Law of Divine Love correctly in our daily lives, we can change the world.

Each of us has come to Earth to learn how to express unconditional love in all that we do and say. We are here to demonstrate to others how God's love can create Heaven on Earth, filling all our lives with love, joy, happiness, peace, health and prosperity. Through love we awaken within ourselves our own God-nature, our divine perfection. Through divine unconditional love we are able to release the illusions of the Earth, all the negative thought forms created by mankind through the misuse of free will, and accept the reality of God and goodness in all things, including each of us.

To effectively begin working with the Law of Divine Love, it is important to fully understand the feeling of unconditional love and trace it to its source — God. The following meditation will help you connect to God's love.

The Spiral of Light Meditation

Sit in a comfortable position, spine straight and take a few very deep breaths. Relax your body more and more with each breath.

Focus your attention on your Heart Chakra in the center of your chest. Imagine or feel a beautiful crystal clear flame in your heart — God's flame. Feel this flame as love.

Now imagine the flame being contained within a tube that runs up and down in the center of your body. Inside this tube create two spirals of crystal-clear liquid light. One spiral moves clockwise, the other, counterclockwise. The spirals move up and down within the tube and in and out.

From your heart, move the spirals all the way up through and beyond the top of your heart, until you feel the presence of God. God's love will be felt like a soft, warm blanket. Feel the love.

The Pyramid of Love Meditation

This meditation is designed for a group of three or more participants.

Sit in a circle with your spine very straight. Begin to breathe deeply, relaxing all parts of your body as you breathe. Place your hands on your thighs and let your mind be empty of all thoughts. As thoughts come in, imagine them drifting out on a soft, pink cloud.

Let's build a pyramid of love. Imagine a golden thread of light coming from your heart and going into the heart of the person sitting on your left in the circle. Now imagine another golden thread of light coming from your heart, connecting to the heart of the person sitting just on the other side of the person to whom you sent the first thread of light. Keep sending out threads of light until everyone in the circle is connected to each other at the heart center.

Focus your attention on your Third Eye. Imagine a beautiful dark-blue thread coming from your Third Eye and connecting to the Third Eye of the person on your left. Then send another blue thread to the next person sitting on the other side of the first person to whom you sent the first blue thread. Send the blue thread to each person in the circle until each is connected to the other, Third Eye to Third Eye.

Imagine you are sitting in a very large pyramid of love, God's love. Imagine God's love coming down from the top of the pyramid as white light. This white light moves out and connects to each participant in the circle at your crown, the top of your head. As before, imagine you are connecting this white light from your crown to each person in the circle, one after the other, until all are connected.

We are all connected to one another in God's love within the circle and pyramid. Let's chant very softly . . . Ommmmmmm. Send the Ommmmmm down the threads of light we have built, first down the golden threads from our hearts, then down the blue threads from our Third Eyes, and finally down our white threads from the crowns of our heads. Feel the love, peace and happiness we have all created together in the pyramid of love.

The OM sound opens our minds and hearts to the vibration of God and God's universe. It helps us connect on a deeper level to God. Chant Ommmmm as long as you wish. You will feel the beautiful loving vibrations of God within you and all around you as you chant.

When you feel ready, open your eyes and be present in the room. Keep feeling the beautiful love we have created within ourselves, in this room and within the universe. Let this love be a part of each of us wherever we go and in whatever we do.

The following meditation is also designed to help us feel unconditional love. It can be done in a group setting or redesigned a bit for individual work.

The Circle of Love Meditation

Sit on the floor or in chairs that have been set up in a circle. Join hands and close your eyes. Take a very deep breath. Let the breath fill your abdomen, then your stomach, chest and finally up to the top of your head. Now hold your breath for a moment, then let it out slowly, from the top of your head down through your chest, stomach and abdomen. Keep breathing very slowly and deeply, allowing your body to relax as though you were floating on top of water or on top of a soft, pink cloud of love.

As you breathe, relax your toes, feet, legs, knees, thighs, hips, abdomen and stomach. Relax your chest and shoulders, down into your arms, hands, fingers and thumbs. Relax your neck, face and head.

As you breathe, imagine a beautiful big pink light coming from God down through the top of your heads and into your whole body. All you can feel is this very special love. You see, God loves us all the time no matter who we are, what we feel or believe or how we act. God is always sending us love, but sometimes we are so busy doing other things we can't feel it. When we are quiet, we can feel God's love more easily. Meditation brings us a time of quiet.

Feel God's love inside your body. Feel the warmth and love in your heart. Feel God all around you as warm, tingling, loving energy. Concentrate on the word "love." Think about how love feels, how good it feels when we receive love from our family and friends, from our pets. Think about how good it feels to give love to others.

Send this love energy to the person sitting on your right side. Think of this love energy as a strong, pink rope. Imagine this pink rope extending from your heart to the heart of the person on your right until the rope extends all around the circle. As you send love around the circle, you are creating a circle of love. The circle of love is made up of energy that makes you feel connected to each person in the circle. When we are connected to one another in love, we feel as though we are one big family — and we are.

Each of us is separate and special, an individual soul, but the energy of love helps us all join together as one wonderful, loving family. You can feel this oneness in the circle now.

As we send love to each other, our energy fills the entire circle, the center of the circle and the room. We have created this love energy with our thoughts and feelings. By thinking and feeling love, we create love. This love energy will stay in the room and make us feel warm and special.

We want to feel good about ourselves and other people. We want to build happy, joyful, loving thoughts rather than thoughts that make us feel unhappy or angry. There are many ways we can use loving thoughts to make the energy change from unhappy to happy, joyful, loving energy.

We can meditate and go inside ourselves to the God within. We can ask and receive help with our work in school, in our friendships, in our relationships with our family. If there is a problem with a teacher, friend or family member, we can sit quietly, go inside ourselves to that special place in our heart where we talk to God, and ask God for help in sending this person love.

Love is like a wave that goes from one person to another, carrying what is in the love-giver's consciousness and bringing the consciousness of the giver and receiver closer into thinking and feeling alike, changing negative emotions to positive emotions. The following exercise will demonstrate how this works.

Exercise to Send and Receive Love

Choose a friend or family member to work with. Sit close together facing each other. One person should be the sender, the other the receiver. The sender now fills his/her Heart Chakra with God's love, visualizing love coming down from God through the top of the head and into the heart. Then the sender flows the love energy from his/her heart to the heart of the receiver, heart to heart.

Did the receiver feel the loving energy? If so, how did it feel? If not, try this exercise again. Sometimes it takes practice to feel the energy.

Now change positions. The receiver becomes the sender, the sender becomes the receiver.

How many times have we found ourselves in a situation where a friend was very angry toward us or accused us of something we did not do. How do we feel when this situation occurs?

Sometimes we feel very helpless. We do not understand what is happening or how to heal the situation. We might react in anger or make our own accusations to get even. Anger feeds anger. Thus our friend would only become more angry, perhaps even striking out at us.

We do not allow anger to pull us out of balance at any time in our life experience. We simply must focus on God's love within us and use it as a tool to change the situation, to transmute the energy.

Exercise in Sending Love to Melt Anger

Close your eyes and sit quietly, relaxing your body as you breathe. Visualize the person who is angry. Or, if he/she is actually standing physically in front of you, close your eyes for a moment to break the flow of angry energy.

Imagine God's love coming down through the top of your head and filling your whole body with love. Send this love from your Heart Chakra to the individual. Send more and more love. Even if that person gets more angry at first, pushes you or yells at you, send more love. Be quiet. Be patient. In a few moments the individual will no longer be feeling or expressing anger, but will forget what he/she was angry about, perhaps even laughing at the whole situation and walking away. Either way, you are finished with the situation.

Now forgive the person and yourself. Imagine the energy being released in a large spiral of energy moving clockwise and counterclockwise at the same time. The spiral moves up and down and takes the unwanted energy of the emotion from the situation, drawing it up to God where it is transmuted into love and light and recycled into other forms of energy.

LOVING OURSELVES

Each of us was created in the image of God, in divine perfection, in divine love. God loves us so much that He/She created for us a beautiful place on Earth in which to experience the physical world, free will and Earth school lessons. Before coming to Earth we have each been given the opportunity to choose our family, our lessons, which sex, country, culture and belief system we wish to be born into, all for the purpose of learning and growing in God's loving light and sharing with those beings who are not in physical body the lessons we learn, for they too are learning through teaching, guiding and serving us.

In coming to Earth we have become involved in the consciousness of this third-dimensional world where there are many thought forms not of God's creation. God created this world based on divine love, where everyone and everything lived in balance and harmony — that was God's intent from the beginning, forever. Through our own misuse of the gift of free will we received from God before coming to Earth, we have learned to exist separately from God and God's love. We listen to people's voices instead of God's voice. We believe in disease, lack, working hard, disharmony and discord rather than happiness, joy, peace, love, harmony, health and prosperity.

At some time, somewhere in the maze of Earth consciousness, we lost touch with the universal laws, with God's energy of equality, oneness, unity. We began to judge others and even ourselves. We began to see some people as less than or better than ourselves. We turned away from the spiritual path in favor of the material world and all the things available to us here. For many of us, that very special loving connection with God seems to be missing from our lives. When love is missing, we feel empty and alone.

It is important to note that before we can truly love anyone or anything else in the universe, we must first love ourselves. Love begins in our own heart and expands outward. If we try to love someone or something else and we do not feel loving toward ourselves, that love we express will not be unconditional but will be dotted with those negative feelings we express toward ourselves. The love we share with others will not be pure.

Loving ourselves is not always easy. We often judge ourselves for small, insignificant things such as, "I should have worn a blue shirt instead of a green one. How stupid!" We often complain about being too short or too tall, too fat or too thin, too shy or too outgoing, not pretty or handsome enough, not creative enough and on and on. The more we complain about our appearance or personality and the more we judge ourselves by seeing what is wrong instead of what is right with us, the less we can express unconditional love for ourselves. When we do not love ourselves, we cannot be truly happy or express our joy and love to others.

Often we can compliment others on how nice they look, how happy they are, how great they make us feel, but when it comes to ourselves, we cannot find the words to say positive things. *What we think, we create.* Thus if we say to ourselves, "You are too fat," we reinforce the weight problem we see ourselves as having. However, if we say, "You are the perfect weight," even if we choose to lose five pounds, the weight will simply balance out. The five pounds will simply drop away in a very short time. Positive and loving thoughts create loving, positive results.

Exercise

Stand in front of your mirror. Look at yourself closely. How do you feel about yourself? What do you see that you like in yourself? What do you see you would like to change in yourself? Why?

As you stand in front of the mirror, do you lovingly examine yourself, noting and appreciating all of your own wonderful God-qualities, or do you criticize and judge yourself? What God-qualities do you see in yourself? Write them down.

As you stand in front of the mirror, look yourself straight in the eye in the reflection in the glass and say, "[your name], I love you. You are very special. God loves you. You are perfect in every way. You cannot be like anyone else because God made you to be different from everyone else, yet you are always a part of Him/Her. I love and accept you just as you are. You are perfect. I love you."

Do this exercise every day, anytime you feel sad, lonely or unloved. You might find this exercise a bit difficult at first, because we do not often find it easy to love ourselves. However, the more this exercise is practiced, the more you will feel that you truly deserve love and that you do, in fact, love yourself. As you love yourself more and more, you will express more unconditional love to others and to the Earth. You will see the difference in your life experience.

ERASING FEAR WITH LOVE

We have learned to be afraid of so many things here on the Earth plane. For some people there is a fear of death, fear of failure, fear of being punished. Some people fear God, fear being abandoned, rejected, not being wanted, being alone. Some people fear loss or not having enough money or losing their job or home. Some people fear illness or surgery. Many people fear the future, the unknown.

Fear is, in truth, an absence of light, an absence of God's love. Fear is a thought we create in our own conscious mind from television programs we watch, from something someone has said, or from what we create in our own imagination. The more thought energy we give to our fear, the greater the fear grows, until the fear encompasses our everyday experiences. For example, fear of the dark can come up every night. As night falls, we become afraid that something will hurt us, that something is there that we cannot see. Many of us have learned certain fears from childhood adventures, from our parents, family members, teachers and friends.

For example:

"Watch out for strangers. One might hurt you."

"Don't touch the stove; you might get burned."

"Stay in bed. Don't get up after I turn out the light. You might bump into something in the dark and hurt yourself."

"The world is such a horrible place. No matter how hard you work, you just never get ahead. You can never have what you want."

"Stay away from 'those' people. You might catch a disease"

Have you ever heard anyone say one or more of these statements or something similar? How do you feel when you read these statements? Do they create in you a bit of fear about strangers, hot stoves, the dark, the world in which we live, and catching a disease?

It takes strength and courage to face your fears. Sometimes it is much easier to see what other people around you are afraid of, rather than look at your own fears. When you look at a friend or family member, you can often see something in them that you are learning about yourself, a fear or some other emotion. The other person reflects to you something you need to see and learn for yourself, something you need to heal and release. It is easier to see things in other people (what is "wrong" with others) rather than within ourselves. This is the reason certain people appear in our lives. They come to show us what we need to learn about ourselves.

Exercise

Think of one of your friends. Look at this friend closely. What do you feel this friend is here to teach you about yourself? Do you see something this friend is afraid of that you are also afraid of? Do you see something this friend is not afraid of that you are afraid of? Your friend wants to go on the Ferris wheel at the fair. You are afraid of high places. The friend convinces you to go on the Ferris wheel and soon you find out how much fun it is. You feel safe with your friend, safe inside the seat belt. You feel secure. Your friend or family member who loves you unconditionally, lovingly encourages you to release your fear and have fun.

We can look at some area in our life where we have a decision to make. We ask ourselves if there is any reason we do not feel free to decide to do what we want to do. Perhaps there is a fear that there will not be enough time or money, a fear that we cannot make it on our own when we grow up, a fear that other people we love will move away and leave us all alone. When we stop for a moment and think about all the beautiful guardian angels and spirit guides/teachers in the heavens who love and protect us, when we think about God's love and protection, the fears dissolve. God is with us wherever we go. As we connect more and more to God and the angelic guides and teachers, we increase the light and the love within our hearts. The love overpowers the fear. Soon we can even laugh at what we were afraid of even a few minutes before.

Many times we fear something that we feel is going to happen in our future. For example, there is a math test tomorrow and we worry about failing the test because we do not understand the lesson. The more fear we give to the possibility of failure, the more we bring the failure to us in reality. We worry about being punished for failing the test, and we bring that to us as well. What we focus our energy and thoughts on, we create.

All our energy is going into the negative thoughts about "what if I fail, get punished" and so on. Why do we fear something that is not even happening in this moment? Why are we afraid of tomorrow's lessons? Why fear something that we can change immediately with loving, positive thoughts?

Worry, concern and fear are very powerful negative thoughts and emotions. The more energy we give these types of thoughts, the more we experience the results. If we do not project ourselves into the possibility of failure, we are much happier. If we stay in the present moment, right here now, we can change our future.

We cannot change what happened to us yesterday. The energy is gone with the day. Whatever lessons were to be learned, were learned. We can, however, change tomorrow. Tomorrow is not yet here in this moment, but as we think about what we want to create for tomorrow, we create it.

Using the example of the math test, we can see that in order to pass the test we must change our thoughts and create what we want. We ask for extra assistance from our parents and we study. We spend some time breathing to relax our body. We think happy thoughts: "I will successfully pass the math test tomorrow. My parents will be proud of me. I will be proud of myself for doing such a great job." As we think positive words, we create positive energy to help us pass the math test the next day — and we do.

Each of us is the master of our own experiences. Each of us has the power to create our own future by changing whatever we do not want to create in that future. Even if someone tells us what they see for us in our future, that person does not have power over our future — *we* do! As we hear what the other person is saying, we can change that possibility and create what *we* want for ourselves. It is that simple.

Exercise to Dissolve Fear

Breathe deeply, drawing your breath from the abdomen up through the center of your body to the top of your head and back down again, keeping the breath flowing. Focus on your heart. Begin breathing from your heart space until you feel deep feelings coming from there. Fill your heart with a deep feeling of love. See this love as God's love.

Think about one fear that you have. See your fear. Feel your fear. Look right at your fear. Face your fear. Do not turn away from it. Shine God's love from your heart right at your fear. Shine more and more loving light until your fear fades away in the light. All you feel is love, peace and joy. Your fear has dissolved into love and light, transmuted from a negative energy into God's loving energy and light.

Exercise to Thank Fear for Its Lesson

Sit quietly and take a few deep breaths. Let your mind focus on your heart center. Create a crystal-clear flame. See this flame contained within a tube in the center of your body. Within this tube create a spiral of crystal-clear liquid light moving clockwise. Create a second spiral of crystal-clear liquid light moving counterclockwise. The liquid light spirals up and down and in and out at the same time. Feel the spirals of light moving up and down, in and out. Feel them. You do not have to see them.

Move the spirals up, up, up, until you feel a deeper connection to God. Find that place in the energy of God that is your personal space. You came from God and there is one very special place within God's loving energy that is for you and you alone.

Feel God's love. Make the love stronger and stronger, until all you feel is this love.

Let one of your biggest fears come into your consciousness. Think about it. Face your fear. Focus all your attention on the fear. As you look at the fear, what lesson are you learning from the experience? Is the fear teaching you to stand in your own power? To not listen to other people? To make your own decisions? To change whatever you do not like with your own power to create with God whatever you choose? Is the fear related to something that happened in a past life?

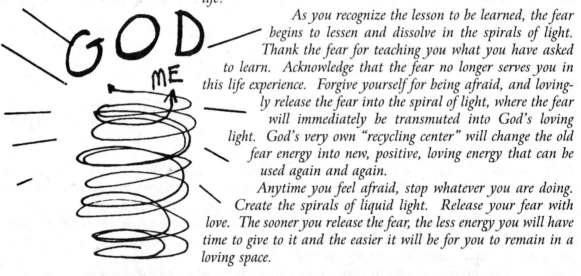

As you recognize the lesson to be learned, the fear begins to lessen and dissolve in the spirals of light. Thank the fear for teaching you what you have asked to learn. Acknowledge that the fear no longer serves you in this life experience. Forgive yourself for being afraid, and lovingly release the fear into the spiral of light, where the fear will immediately be transmuted into God's loving light. God's very own "recycling center" will change the old fear energy into new, positive, loving energy that can be used again and again.

Anytime you feel afraid, stop whatever you are doing. Create the spirals of liquid light. Release your fear with love. The sooner you release the fear, the less energy you will have time to give to it and the easier it will be for you to remain in a loving space.

THROUGH LOVE, WE MAINTAIN PERFECT HEALTH

God is love and perfection. Since we are one with God, our natural state of being is love and perfection. Perfect health is reflected in the state of perfection as reality. Disease is an illusion we create on the Earth plane from a thought.

All disease as we know it on Earth begins with some form of thought in our mental body. What we think about ourselves and our environment becomes part of our emotional body and we begin to feel this thought. If we are not aware of this thought/feeling, the negative energy manifests in our physical body in the form of pain, discomfort or disease.

We often seek the services of a medical professional when we are not feeling well. We go to the doctor where we are examined and perhaps diagnosed as having a certain ailment or problem. The doctor might prescribe medication for this ailment. The medication might cause the physical symptoms to disappear, but what about the thought that created the physical symptoms? If the thought is not corrected and released, the physical symptoms can occur again and again until we pay attention to what our body is trying to teach us.

Whenever there is a pain in the body or an ailment, we need to examine that area of our body and what the pain or ailment is trying to show us. We may develop a pain in our neck. As we take our attention into the pain, we may discover that we had just said about someone, "He is a pain in the neck." What you thought and stated, you created in your body as a lesson.

Cancer is a thought form that makes the statement: "I don't like my body. I don't like myself." Cancer is a form of self-destruction that eats away. Very angry people who do not release the energy of the negative feeling can develop cancer as a result. As the energy around the thought is released, the cancer disappears.

Fear of a certain disease can bring it to us as well. If we fear that we may catch the flu from a friend, we very likely will draw the flu experience to us. The more fear energy we give the situation, the more quickly we will develop the flu. As we stand in our God-power and release any energy we may feel about having the flu, we dissolve the energy and maintain health.

The following exercise can be used in examining the thought form that created any illness or discomfort in our body:

Healing Exercise

Sit quietly and take a few deep breaths. Make sure you are in a place where you will not be disturbed. Go into your heart and create the feeling of a crystal-clear flame of light. See the flame contained within a tube in the center of your body.

Now create two spirals of liquid light. One spiral moves clockwise, and the other, counter-clockwise, up and down and in and out inside the tube you have created.

Move your attention upward in the spiral until you feel the energy of God and you as one. Feel that place in the energy of God that is your place.

Take your attention into the area of your body where you are feeling the pain or discomfort. Ask the place in your body to share with you what you need to see or feel, the lesson you are to learn from the experience. Let the energy come into your consciousness. Is the pain trying to tell you to move in a different direction? To slow down? To get more rest? Is the discomfort showing you a certain emotion that you are holding onto that needs to be released? Is there a lot of confusion about what to do with your life?

You will soon sense the thought that created the discomfort. Simply thank your body for teaching you this lesson. Forgive yourself for holding on to the discomfort and release it into the spiral. Even if there is energy from some other lifetime, it can be released into the spiral and transmuted into love and light. As soon as you recognize what your body is trying to teach you and release the thought, the pain and discomfort will move with it.

As we evolve to that place where we see ourselves in God's perfection, we no longer create disease. We maintain a state of balance in love where we are happy. In the moment when we do not see or feel that perfection, we can re-create the energy of perfection through love. Through the energy of love all imperfection is dissolved.

The Mirror Exercise

Close your eyes and take a few deep breaths. Imagine that you are sitting or standing in front of a large mirror in which you can see your entire body from head to foot.

As you scan your body, think about the positive qualities of God's perfection: joy, love, happiness, balance, harmony, health, abundance. Is there anything that you see in yourself that is not a positive, loving God-quality? Is there anything you see that you find yourself judging or criticizing? Is there a pain or discomfort? Is there an unhappy feeling or thought?

Become aware of those places in your body that do not radiate God-qualities as you perceive them. Fill your heart with love. Let the love become so strong that you can feel only love – nothing from the outside world comes into your awareness. See yourself as perfect in every way. Feel that perfection. Imagine that you have erased all imperfections and affirm: "I am perfect. I am happy, joyful, peaceful, healthy, abundant."

If there is a pain or discomfort in your body, feel the love in your heart begin to build. Take yourself into the pain or discomfort. Ask the pain to tell you or show you what thought or feeling is causing the discomfort. Listen carefully. Soon you will know exactly what the pain is, where it came from and what was said to you.

Thank the pain for teaching you what you needed to learn. Forgive yourself for creating the pain and holding on to the discomfort. Release the pain into the spiral of light. Take a few deep breaths as you release the pain.

Any words or feelings that we hear or sense, any thoughts we feel or believe about ourselves, become our truth. Any negative thought can be created in our body as disease unless we release it quickly. It is important to maintain positive, loving thoughts at all times.

Disease is an illusion; disease does not exist unless we believe in imperfection and allow the disease to manifest in our body. When we believe in perfection, when we know we are one with God, disease will cease to occur. Where there is love, disease cannot exist. Love yourself and create health.

Some positive affirmations to create perfection include:

"I am love. I am loved and worthy of being loved."

"I love and forgive myself for anything I have accepted that is not my truth."

"I love and approve of myself. I do not have to seek approval and love from others."

"I experience life as a loving, happy and joyful opportunity to grow in God's light.

"There is no right or wrong. Life is simply a series of lessons I have chosen to participate in openly and lovingly."

"I am perfect just as I am."

"I express my feelings openly and freely."

"I live in the moment. I cannot change what was. In this very moment I create my future with loving energy."

"I am fully responsible for my own well-being. I cannot fix other people. I stand in my power and do not allow other people to fix me."

"God and I are One. God loves me in all situations. He knows I am doing my best as I learn in the Earth school. God approves of me and accepts me just as I am."

See how many other positive affirmations you can create in a loving way to express divine love. See each affirmation you create as another step up the ladder to greater awareness.

LOVE EQUALS FORGIVENESS

There are times when a friend or family member treats us in a way that makes us so angry or hurt that we begin to feel more and more angry energy inside ourselves. We look at the person with angry thoughts. Every time we see them or think about them, we feel angry. Anger is not an expression of divine love. It is a negative emotion that if not released can only create more and more negative emotions in the person experiencing the anger. If we are angry, our energy field will affect all others we come in contact with. Have you ever walked into a room where someone was very angry? How did you feel? How do you feel when your parents are angry at you?

The longer we hold grudges for something someone said to us, did to us and so on, the more we hold ourselves back from growing in God's love. When we are not expressing and experiencing love of a higher nature, we are not growing and learning as God intends for us. We remain in a state of limbo and we are not happy.

Forgiveness releases the energy. Love is forgiveness. Through forgiveness we correct all misunderstandings that occur in any life experiences. Through forgiveness — love — we free the energy that has been holding us in a state of limbo, and we thus free ourselves. We can then move into the next lesson.

Exercise

Sit in a quiet place and close your eyes. Breathe very deeply and let your body relax as you breathe.

Now think about someone who you feel has hurt you in some way or has made you very angry. Focus your full attention on this person. See the person and the situation that created the negative feelings. What happened? What created the hurt or anger? Did the friend tease you? Did the friend intend to hurt you? If so, why do you feel this way? Did you say or do something you were not even aware of that created the situation?

As you look at the situation and the causes for the anger or hurt, you will begin to see what you are to learn from the experience. Perhaps the lesson has to do with sharing, not judging or criticizing, thinking before speaking, or being patient or loving. As you become aware of the lessons, simply say: "[Person's name], I forgive you. I love you unconditionally and release the negative energy between us. I forgive you now for (say whatever you feel you need to say to forgive the person). I forgive myself for being angry or feeling hurt." Then release the anger or hurtful feelings into the spiral of liquid light. See the negative feelings transmuted into love and light.

Look at anyone or anything that has made you feel angry or hurt. Release anything you are still holding onto in your body. As you release the energy you feel lighter, more loving, free. As you release the energy, fill your heart with love until all you feel in your heart is LOVE.

DAILY THOUGHTS ON LOVE

To experience and express divine love in all that we do, there are a few important points to be aware of and to focus on daily:

Love begins with loving the self. We cannot love anyone else until we first love ourselves. Each of us is a part of God, and God is love. We were created as perfect. We are here to honor that perfection within ourselves at all times. When we criticize something about ourselves, we are not honoring the God within us. We are, in a sense, disapproving of God and all of creation that we are a part of.

To love ourselves means to accept ourselves just as we are without criticism or judgment. Look at yourself in the mirror. What do you see? Do you look for the positive qualities in yourself, such as having a beautiful smile? Or do you look for all the flaws (as they appear to you)? Do you see yourself as anything but perfect? ("My hair is too short; my nose is too long. I am too fat. I am not pretty/handsome.") These are put-downs and do not create positive, loving energy. They do not reflect the energy of loving oneself — and what we think, we create. Thus, as we reflect on these "flaws" in ourselves, we strengthen that energy and create them.

Look in the mirror. Smile and say, "[your name], I love you. You are a perfect reflection of God, perfect in every way, just as you are now. I see the love and light of God within you. I love you." Feel the words as you say them. Feel them in your body and your heart. As you do so, the words reflect a sense of reality in your body cells. Your whole attitude about yourself, other people, the world, begins to change. Try it.

Forgiveness allows more love to flow from our heart. Holding onto old grudges, anger or hurt feelings creates energy blockages that interfere with the flow of love. Negative emotions eventually can create disease in the physical body.

Sit quietly and imagine someone you feel has caused you pain, someone who has taken advantage of you, been deceitful or done something to make you feel unhappy. See the person as clearly as possible in your imagination. Create the double spiral of crystal-clear liquid light and move the energy up and down and in and out. Feel the spiral inside the center of your body moving up higher and higher into the energy of God.

Let the word, thought, feeling or emotion come into your conscious mind. Whatever you feel you need to say to this individual, let the energy come into your awareness. Speak verbally directly to the image you have created. Speak from your heart and release everything you have stuffed inside since the time when the situation occurred.

When you are finished, say, "[Person's name], I forgive you with total, unconditional love from my heart. I see our experience together as a lesson I have chosen to learn. You have helped me learn an important lesson. I thank you for assisting me. I now forgive myself for holding on to this emotion. I thank the experience for coming into my awareness. I now release this emotion and I am free."

With the release of this old energy, you are now ready to experience a new, more positive lesson. As we release the past, the old emotions, we can grow and move forward.

Love is accepting everyone as equals, without judgment or discrimination. When you look at a person who seems to struggle all or most of the time and who has very little to fulfill his/her needs, then you look at another who seems to be getting everything and more than they need without putting out much effort (as you see it), release immediately any feelings of judgment or discrimination. See each of these individuals for who they truly are — a soul in the family of God. Each person is here to learn an important lesson. We cannot take responsibility for other people's lessons. However, we can honor them by recognizing their own individual need to experience an important lesson they have chosen to learn.

We are each a part of God's family. We are all brothers and sisters, no matter who we are, what we believe, where we live, what color our skin or what we choose as lessons.

We are responsible only for our own happiness and joy. We are not responsible for the happiness and well-being of anyone else on the planet or in the universe. Our only responsibility is to love ourselves, to be loved, to transmit love to the Earth and to all of creation. We are not here to judge or discriminate, for these are thoughts that will create judgment and discrimination upon ourselves. We are here to allow each soul to participate in the game of life as they see fit.

Love heals, balances and harmonizes. Love creates unity, oneness. We are each working now toward the goal of unity and love for the Earth and all of creation.

Love brings peace and freedom. When we come from a loving space as we deal with situations, we send out loving thoughts to others, to the Earth. Love goes out in waves and creates more love around us. As we send out more and more love, we soon find we are at peace with ourselves and the world. We feel free of any negative emotion.

When we express love in all situations, we avoid creating negative thoughts, feelings and emotions. Through the expression of love we maintain balance and harmony, the foundation upon which the universe was created. If there is nothing to reflect back to us but love, we remain in a state of peace. When we do not create negative thoughts and emotions, we remain *free* of having to deal with such emotions on any level. Our energy can then be spent on a more positive experience of growth and learning.

Love is all there is. God is all there is. Everything we see in form came from God's love. Thus love is everywhere in all things, in all beings.

Fear, anger, hate, greed, doubt and the like are not the products of divine love, but rather are thoughts and feelings that often mask or hide that love within us. Negative thoughts can never truly destroy the love that each of us is, because love is who we are. There are times when we are very unhappy or angry and we do not feel very loving, yet we must always remember that love is contained within us, in our heart, and all we have to do is go into our heart and feel that love, feel God.

Love is the most powerful emotion/vibration in the universe because love *is* God. Where there is love there can be no darkness, no disease, no disharmony. Since fear, anger, hate, greed, resentment and so on are all negative forms of energy, and negative energy is seen as darkness, where love is felt and expressed they cannot exist. Love your fear. Love your anger. Send love from your heart to any negative thought, feeling or emotion. Then love and forgive yourself for holding on to such emotions.

Fear will turn to laughter. Love your anger and anger will turn to friendship. Love your doubts and they will become faith. Love your greed; it will become sharing. LOVE HEALS EVERYTHING. LOVE IS ALL THERE IS.

Many wonderful books have been written on the subject of love. Perhaps you would like to write one yourself? Perhaps there is a story to tell, or a poem. When you think of love, think of God. When you think of God, think of yourself. We are, in truth, one family of loving souls in God's light, learning and sharing together.

DEMONSTRATING UNCONDITIONAL LOVE THROUGH INVOLVEMENT

There are many ways to demonstrate unconditional love. The following activities are but a few:

- Share your love by volunteering your service in hospitals, hospices, day care for children and adults, convalescent homes or places where people need a little love and some warm hugs.
- Adopt a pet and share your love with an animal that is homeless. Animals teach us all about loyalty and unconditional love, which is their specialty. Even if an animal's owner is unkind to it, the animal will still express love to the abusive owner. Love teaches us to turn the other cheek, to love the aggressor. As we share our love unconditionally and without expectation in all situations, we receive back even more than we have given.
- Joyfully offer to help with chores at home. Work without expectation of payment for your service. You will be surprised at the many rewards you will receive for your unselfish efforts.
- Make a "best friend" out of a new student at school, a new neighbor or someone who seems shy or alone. Sometimes this person will become your best friend. You will never know how great a friend this individual could be unless you introduce yourself and get to know him or her.
- Share your allowance with others you feel you would like to help. Even a small percentage of your allowance can bring you more money in return for your unselfish sharing with others.
- Collect extra canned and boxed food products from your neighbors and donate it to the food bank in your neighborhood. Providing food for hungry people is a special sharing of love.

There are many more activities you can get involved in. Gather some friends together and see what ideas you can come up with. Share the experience of loving those who need a little extra comfort and support.

When we can each truly learn the Law of Divine Love and apply this law in all our experiences — in our actions, thoughts, feelings, expressions — we will develop a feeling of unity that will make us feel loved and connected to all of creation. The YOU-ME feeling of separateness will dissolve into the WE feeling of connectedness. As the merger takes place, as we begin to see each other as equals and truly care about the well-being of each other, we create a deeper, stronger connection to God and to all of creation.

Divine love is a healing force so powerful that it will eliminate all thoughts, feelings and emotions that are not in harmony with God's plan. As we incorporate divine love into our daily lives, we will find peace, joy, security, health, happiness. Love is the beginning. Love has no end. Love is in all things equally at all times. Become aware of that love within yourself. Be love!

AFFIRMATION: Love is at the center of my being in my heart. Love is who I am. Love brings me peace, joy, happiness, balance, harmony, health and prosperity. Love flows freely through every part of me. Love frees me of any thoughts, feelings and emotions that are not of love. Through divine love, I again experience my oneness, my divine totality. God and I are one in love.

8 • THE LAW OF HARMONY

God created the universe and all living things within it to love and respect each other's space, value and life experience, without focusing on competition, greed and selfishness. Each living thing was created to live in harmony with one another, each part of creation in balance with the other, each working together for the good of the whole.

The word "harmony" can be defined as a state of balance and equality, where all things existing in a certain area work together to create for the entire area a state of unity and peace. Wherever harmony is established, there can exist no conflict, discord, disharmony or disease.

The Law of Harmony states that each part of creation must be in harmony and balance with other parts of the universe. If one part of creation is out of balance and harmony, it affects all the other parts.

Harmony is a blending of energies like the blending of voices in a choir. If we were to separate the individuals singing in a choir, for example, we would find that each person not only looks different physically and has different beliefs and practices, but also has a different-sounding, unique voice, or tone.

A choir is made up of several different tonal ranges that we group into bass, tenor, alto and soprano, which move from very low and deep to very high. Within these basic groups voices vary in tonal quality. Some bass voices, for example, are much lower and deeper than others, and each singer in the bass section expresses a different quality of sound. Singers with a very high soprano voice often sing in the opera, reaching notes so high and with such perfection that many of us are wonderstruck at such a gifted singer.

The blending of these voices, tones or sounds is called harmonizing. All the voices create together an energy that blends and makes beautiful music, and it can be much more pleasing than one single voice alone.

We have labeled the various musical tones or notes. A keyboard or any other musical instrument has a tonal range from its low notes to its high notes that creates the music we wish to play. If you have a piano available, begin at the left side of the keyboard and strike the keys. On this end of the piano you will find the bass (very low) sounds. As you move to the right, the notes are increasingly higher.

Watch a musician play the piano. Several keys are usually played at the same time, creating a chord. Chords are a blend of notes that create the beautiful harmony of a song. If you have a keyboard instrument, try placing your fingers on various keys or strings to see how the sounds affect you when you create a harmonious chord or play notes that seem to blend. How do you feel when you play a chord in which one or more notes do not blend and are not in harmony?

Each part of creation has its own musical note or harmonic tone that brings it into balance and harmony with all the rest of creation. Each of us has a specific tone or note that is unique, and each of our chakras vibrates to a specific note of the musical scale.

Exercise to Feel Sound in the Chakras

For this exercise you will need a keyboard, or a tape of the particular musical notes listed in the exercise: C, D, E, F#, G#, high A and high B.

Sit quietly and breathe deeply to relax your body. As you breathe, release all tension in your body. Play the note C as you focus on your Root Chakra at the base of your spine. Feel the vibration of the note in your chakra. Let the energy expand and create harmony in this center.

Say the sound "eh" (as in the word "red"). Repeat "eh" at least three times while focusing on the Root Chakra.

Now, move your attention to the Second Chakra in the center of your abdomen. Imagine the color orange as you play the note D. Feel its vibration in your Second Chakra.

Say the sound "oh" (as in "home"). Repeat "oh" at least three times while focusing on your Second Chakra.

Focus on your Third Chakra just above your navel and imagine a bright yellow energy center.

Play the note E and feel the vibration in this center.

Say the sound "ahh–ooo–mmm" and repeat three times while focusing in this center.

Bring your attention to your Heart Chakra in the center of your chest and imagine a bright green center. Play the note F# and feel the vibration in your heart.

Say the sound "ah," repeating it at least three times. How does the energy feel in your Heart Chakra?

Move your attention to your Throat Chakra and play the musical note G#. Feel the vibration of the G# there. Now repeat the sound "oo" (as in "blue") at least three times. Feel this sound in your throat. How does your Throat Chakra feel now?

Bring your attention to your Third Eye in the center of your forehead. Play the note high A. Feel the vibration of this note in your Third Eye. Now repeat the sound "ee" (as in the word "bee") for a minimum of three times. Feel the vibration. Does your Third Eye feel more open and balanced?

Now move to your Crown Chakra at the top of your head. Play the note high B. Feel the note's vibration at the top of your head.

Chant the sound "OM" several times. Feel your entire body vibrate as it comes into balance and harmony with the energy of God's universe.

When all parts of creation blend through their own balanced harmonic tones, there is HARMONY. If a single part of creation is not in harmony within itself, it does not blend with the whole, and all other parts of creation are affected. This is the basis of the Law of Harmony.

If we strike a note on a musical instrument that is out of sequence with the other notes being played, the notes do not blend. An irritating sound is created. This one note that is not in harmony can change the harmonic balance of the entire song.

Exercise to feel Disharmonious Sounds

One very familiar example of creating disharmony through sound involves writing on a blackboard with a piece of chalk and another object. The chalk creates a soft sound on the board as words are written. The sound is comfortable to the human ear. But what happens if your fingernail or another solid object suddenly slips across the board? How does the sound make you feel? We can say that the sound of the chalk on the board is in harmony with our energy field, but the sound of the other object (or fingernail) is not.

In accepting separateness and duality rather than connectedness and oneness, humans have chosen to spend time "doing their own thing." Often we find ourselves involved in something that is not in harmony with other people in our family, in our circle of friends, in our neighborhood and so on. For example, we might rise at the same time as another family member and want to use the bathroom at the same time. We have a conflict over who is going to take a shower first, who is going to use this hair dryer or that one, and on and on. Perhaps we rise at 6 a.m. and decide to mow the lawn, without giving consideration to the neighbor who works late at night. This experience is not in harmony because the energies do not blend and work together. To blend, we would have to come to an agreement about sharing the bathroom or mowing the lawn.

There are people on the Earth who always want to be first, to be the leader, to get ahead of all the rest of the people. There are people who do not tell the truth and who create disharmony through their deceit. There are people who would rather steal from others to get what they want; their actions are certainly not in harmony with the people they steal from.

In large businesses and corporations, people compete with one another for positions of power. If one individual does not receive a promotion, he/she may resent it and work against the person who does get the job. There are often many conflicts in the workplace, and there is certainly disharmony.

We experience disharmony in the world. One country does not want to trade with another country. One group of people does not want to share with another. Everywhere we look in the world today, we can observe much disharmony. Disharmony is created by our wanting to be better than someone else, by wanting more power, more possessions. Disharmony is created from separateness.

Exercise in Noticing Disharmony

Go through the newspapers and magazines. Clip out different articles that you feel are related to disharmony. Make note of any television programs you see or newscasts and so on where disharmony is evident.

Now make a scrapbook or journal of those events and situations you have discovered that relate to disharmony. Next to the article or journal entry, paste a picture or another article/entry of a situation that would create harmony. For example, if you cut out an article on war, you might find an article on a peace demonstration or movement. The war is disharmonious, and the peace movement is bringing a state of harmony to the Earth.

Each of us as souls has been created to exist in harmony with God's perfection. We are LOVE. We were created from love and we exist in love. When we are in a loving space, we are in harmony with God and all of creation because all of creation is based on love.

Love is the glue that holds all parts of creation together as one. When we are not coming from a loving space, we are not in harmony with God and with all other parts of creation. When we are not in a loving space, we are in a state of disharmony and imbalance. Our life experience then becomes unhappy. We are faced with obstacles and limitations that we create for ourselves. We feel sad, lonely, resentful, depressed. We cannot see our perfection. We judge and criticize ourselves and other people. Our life seems to work against us rather than for our benefit. In this state of disharmony, we can develop disease. Disease begins with a negative thought which itself begins from a state of disharmony within us.

The comparison between states of harmony and disharmony will offer more clarity about these two states of being.

Any state of negativity is not in harmony with God's law. Let's compare the number of ways we as human beings create harmony of disharmony in our own lives. Whatever we create for ourselves, according to the Law of Harmony, affects all parts of creation.

HARMONY	DISHARMONY
• We love all things and all beings equally. We see all of creation as part of God and therefore part of us. We are all brothers and sisters in God's family.	• We judge and discriminate. We see one group of people as better than others. We feel separate from others.
• We trust in God and have faith that all our needs are met at all times. We can create anything we need.	• We are insecure. We fear loss of home, job, family, friends, loved one(s), our life.
• We live in the moment, realizing that now, in this moment, we are creating our future. No one has power over us. We create our own future from what we think and believe.	• We fear tomorrow and the future. We worry about things that aren't here yet. What if I fail in school? What if my dad loses his job? and so on.

HARMONY

- We appreciate all the wonderful things God has given us. We are willing to share our things with others.
- We create our own life experiences. We have the power to change what we do not wish to have in our life.
- Change allows us to move closer to God. Change brings new and more positive experiences into our lives. We become more loving and happy.

DISHARMONY

- We don't have enough. Others have so much more than we have. We need more. We don't care how we get it.
- It is our parents' fault we are as we are. Perhaps we deserve the bad things that happen to us. God doesn't love us.
- We fear change. We don't want to lose our friends and family. We are comfortable where we are. If we change, we might be unhappy.

How many other thoughts can you make note of that create harmony or disharmony in your own life? How are the thoughts of disharmony affecting you? Your friends? Your family? Your community? The Earth as a whole? God's universe?

Each living thing has a job to do and a lesson it has chosen to learn in the Earth school. No one part of creation is less than or has less value or importance than the others, for each has come from the same source of all life — God. Each has been created from God's love and is that love. Each of us is one with all others. None of the parts work effectively alone, for each affects the other. When in balance and harmony, each part affects the other in a positive, harmonious way. When out of balance, each affects the other in a negative, disharmonious way.

God's creations have been classified into what we call kingdoms. The plant, animal, mineral and human kingdoms are each here to learn to work together in balance and harmony, each bringing something of great value to teach and share with the other kingdoms, one learning from the other.

The **mineral kingdom** is the foundation on which we build our homes on the Earth. This kingdom provides homes not only for mankind, but for other living creatures. From this kingdom is created the soil that is home to the plant kingdom. Animals and insects find holes or burrows in the rock where they can be safe and warm. The mineral kingdom also provides us with certain supplements our bodies need to stay healthy, such as iron, zinc, copper, magnesium and so on.

The **plant kingdom** provides homes, oxygen and food for many of God's creation. The insect world cares for the plants, pollinating the various species, protecting many plants from disease and predators, and helping to mulch the soil for good growth. Insects provide certain nutrients to the soil to help plants maintain good health.

The plant kingdom provides herbs used in medicines. It is believed that for every disease known to mankind there is a plant or herb to help with the healing process. Trees and plants provide fresh oxygen for the air we breathe. Without oxygen, we would all perish from the Earth.

The **animal kingdom** teaches us unconditional love and loyalty. Some animals serve as a method of transportation. Most of the Indians and cowboys relied on horses to travel about. In many countries of the world today, cattle are used to plow the fields. Animals provide food and clothing. They teach us how to survive in the world and indicate to us when harsh weather is approaching. Have you ever noticed an animal's behavior when an earthquake was approaching?

Each animal teaches us a spiritual lesson. The ant teaches us about patience and working together in community. The beaver teaches us to build a strong foundation for our home. The deer teaches us gentleness. The rabbit shows us how to deal with fear. The porcupine teaches us not to judge things from the outside. (A porcupine looks very threatening on the outside with all its sharp quills, but on the inside she is very loving and gentle.)

Exercise

Create a journal of those things you learn from different animals. Find a picture of the animal you are writing about to remind you of its special qualities and paste it in your journal.

The animal kingdom fertilizes the soil for the plants, and together help break up rocks to create new soil and nutrients. Animals help thin out areas of thick foliage. Can you think of other ways animals work together with the plant, mineral and human kingdoms?

The **human kingdom** was created to work with these other kingdoms, learning to share and to use only what they needed to survive. Mankind was created to love all things equally and to teach the other kingdoms about love, to help each one evolve to a higher place in God's kingdom. Mankind was given "dominion" over the other kingdoms, meaning that humans were put in charge of their care to assure all kingdoms they would live in peace, love and abundance. This dominion did not mean that mankind was given power to dominate the other kingdoms.

If we were to eliminate the one kingdom that has brought imbalance to the Earth, which kingdom would it be? Yes, the human kingdom. Mankind has not maintained balance and harmony in the world. Through free will, mankind began to want more for itself, giving little concern to the balance of nature, to the needs of the other parts of creation. People began to pollute the air and streams, killing trees and plant life as well as the creatures who inhabited the areas they destroyed through their lack of concern. Mankind began to take metals and other resources from the Earth, leaving large holes and weak areas where the ground has caved in and where the soil has become barren, no longer useful for growing crops or harboring animal life.

Mankind has created nuclear waste, which remains active for millions of years. This toxic waste threatens the very existence of this planet for many generations to come. Mankind seems to have little concern for the Earth and what may happen if these imbalances are not corrected.

Often we look at the situation on Earth and feel that the task is so great that we could not possibly make a difference. It is important to note, however, that each one of us can make a difference. The time is *now*. If each one of us begins to work on improving the Earth's condition, we will see a great difference.

Exercise to Create an Earth Mandala

Using a large piece of butcher paper or poster board, draw a picture of the Earth. From magazines, brochures and newspapers, cut out pictures that represent the Earth in balance. For example, cut out pictures that show clean, clear lakes and oceans; tall, fresh, green trees; fields of flowers; people dancing or playing together and the like. Let this picture become a mandala for your focus in a special Earth healing meditation that you can do alone or with a group.

Remember, as you do the following meditation, that whatever you focus your attention on, you create. By thinking positive, loving thoughts about the Earth and her people, you create harmony and healing for the Earth. In return, you receive love back. Whatever we give out, we receive back ten times greater.

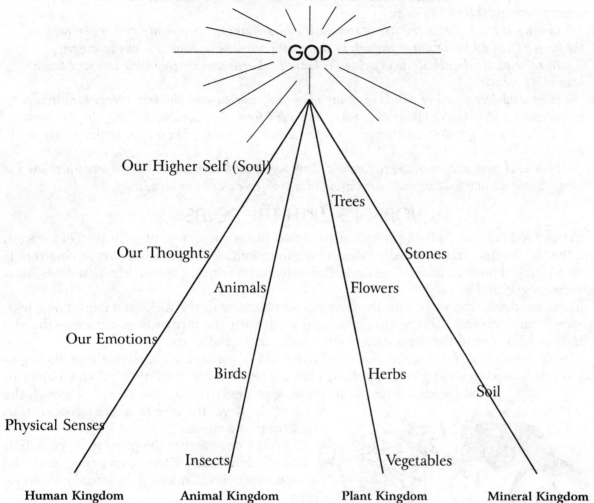

ALL IS ONE IN GOD'S UNIVERSE

GOD

Our Higher Self (Soul)

Trees

Our Thoughts

Stones

Animals

Flowers

Our Emotions

Birds

Herbs

Soil

Physical Senses

Insects

Vegetables

Human Kingdom   **Animal Kingdom**   **Plant Kingdom**   **Mineral Kingdom**

Earth Healing Meditation

Tape your Earth Healing poster to the wall or stand it against the wall so it can become your focus point as you begin to breathe deeply. As you focus attention on the beautiful Earth poster you have created, imagine God's white light coming down through the top of your head and into your arms and hands. You will begin to sense a warmth in your hands as you concentrate on bringing God's light into your body.

Now reach your arms up over your head and place your flat palms together, making a little circle. Concentrate on the inside of this circle. Imagine a golden light of healing energy glowing brighter and brighter, beginning to fill this entire space.

Soon you will feel a warm, glowing energy filling the space within the circle you have created with your arms and hands. You will feel this energy becoming stronger and stronger. As you open your hands, feel this healing energy and imagine it floating up and out into the environment. With your mind, direct the energy to flow into the air we breathe, the animals, plants, the lakes and streams, rivers and oceans, the rocks and soil, to all the people of the Earth. See the energy touch the entire Earth, each part of creation.

See the Earth glow in a golden light as the healing begins to take place. Create a picture of the Earth in your mind, a picture of the fresh, new Earth. Imagine healthy green trees, fresh and strong, and beautiful lush green plants.

Imagine fresh, clean water in all the oceans, lakes, rivers and streams, with plenty of fresh water for all living things to enjoy.

Imagine the rich, fertile soil free of chemicals and pollutants. See plenty of crops growing in the fields to feed all living things, enough to share with everyone equally. No one is hungry.

Imagine plentiful animal life enjoying the beautiful Earth and sharing their love and lessons with all of mankind.

Now send love to all of mankind, imagining men, women and children everywhere living in harmony and balance, taking only what they need from the Earth and living simply, happily without fear, greed or selfishness. See the Earth at peace. The Earth smiles as she is healed.

Now send more and more love to yourself. Love begins with each of us. Let the love from God bring your body into balance and harmony. Open your eyes as you feel ready.

WORKING WITH THE DEVAS

When God created all living things, a deva was placed in charge of each part of creation from the tiniest grain of sand to the tallest tree and mountain. A deva is a part of God that is not in a physical body or form. The devic family includes fairies, gnomes, elves, undines, salamanders, angels and so on.

There are devas who work with the flowers and plants, with the rocks and mountains, with the oceans and streams. There are devas who work with the elements of nature — the elementals — who control the wind, rain, snow, earthquakes and so on.

The fairy of a rose, for instance, has the loving task of caring for a rosebush from its beginning as a tiny seed to a full-grown flowering plant. The deva has the flower's divine blueprint and guides the rose in its growing process from seed to flower. Through the work of the deva, the rose becomes a rose instead of a tulip or a stone.

As the deva assists the plant in its growth, it learns about the Earth experience and the importance of maintaining balance and harmony.

Through the desire to improve upon nature and what God has created, mankind has changed the divine blueprints of many animals and plants by crossbreeding them in laboratories, farms and gardens. Mankind has developed chemicals to destroy the harmful insects, but which kill all insects, many of which are here to protect the crops.

The devas have become confused because the living thing they are in charge of no longer fits the divine blueprint that God had created. Some devas are so upset that they are no longer caring for the Earth. Thus the Earth is no longer in harmony with the plan devised at beginning of creation. Many living things are disappearing from the Earth or are no longer useful to the harmony and balance of this planet.

The devas need to know we love and care about them, that we feel their work is important and that we want to help them. Every living thing on Earth has a deva in charge of its growth and well-being. Thus by loving all things equally, by caring for all devas and that part of creation they are caring for, we can help restore harmony once more to the Earth.

The devas feel too that it is important for us to see or feel their presence. The following meditation will help you contact the devas in your own yard or garden; it is an important exercise you can teach your family and friends.

Deva Meditation

Sit very quietly and focus your attention on a tree or plant in front of you. Say to yourself, I am one with this plant. I want to communicate lovingly with the nature spirits who take care of this plant. In love and harmony, I want to work with you. I lovingly ask for your help. I lovingly recognize your presence. I believe in you and the work you are doing. I love you and thank you for being here.

Now close your eyes. Imagine you are part of the plant. You are floating into the leaves, down the stem and into the roots. Sense very carefully all the energies of the plant. Pay close attention to the nature spirits of the plant as they lovingly come out so you can see them. You may see, hear or feel them or just know they are there. Listen! What do they have to share with you?

"Now you know how to help other people see us," the deva says, "and know we are really here to help. Love all the plants, animals, rocks and each other. When you love all living things equally, you are loving us, the devic kingdom. Love the angels who watch over you. Thank them for taking such good care of you. In turn, we will love all parts of creation. Together we will all help bring Earth back into harmony and balance."

When mankind came to Earth to learn lessons, each person was given the special assistance of many beautiful guides and teachers who do not have a physical form. One special group of helpers are members of the angelic kingdom, assigned to help each of us learn our lessons. As we learn, they learn through us and we grow in God's love and light — together.

Because angels do not have a physical body as we do, we must use our inner vision to see them. Angels are pure energy of total, unconditional love. They have been created by God to serve Him/Her and to help those of us who come in body to experience the Earth lessons.

Angels speak to one another and oftentimes to us in tones or harmonics. Each angel represents a specific musical note as we do. Their presence helps bring balance and harmony to Earth and to each of the kingdoms, most importantly to the human kingdom.

Angels have many special tasks to perform on the Earth plane:

Angels act as God's messengers. Many times in our life experiences we find ourselves trying to find a solution to some situation that is making us unhappy or distressed. If we become still and ask for assistance from the angels, the solution will come to us easily and quickly. Angels are always ready and willing to help. All we need to do is remember to *ask*.

Angels protect us from harm. Have you ever felt an invisible push to get you out of the way of a car or some other form of danger? Perhaps you wanted to follow your friends across the creek, but something made you feel very uncomfortable about it. You did not go, and you felt good about your decision. Each of us has a guardian angel who watches over us and guides us away from danger. We feel the angel's warnings in our body as a knowing or feeling.

Angels comfort us when we are not feeling well or happy. Because angels are joyful, they want to laugh and play and would like us to laugh and play as well. Anytime we feel ill or unhappy, we can ask our special healing angels to come and help. Angels are very connected to God. As they send their healing light into our bodies, they are acting like a pipe that flows healing light from God into our bodies.

Anytime you are feeling sad or ill, imagine your angels placing their hands wherever you want them to touch your body. Imagine God's healing energy coming from above and flowing through you as white light. Imagine the light flowing directly to that part of your body which is not feeling balanced. You can place your own hands on that part of your body as well and see the healing light energy coming from God through your hands, taking away all the unwanted energy. When you feel better, remove your hands and thank the angels for their loving assistance.

The angels are very good at healing plants and animals, and they will enjoy working with you to heal the Earth.

Angels give us special guidance in our spiritual studies. Many times we are led to a special book or teacher when we have questions to ask about God or some spiritual truth. The angels, who know right where we can find the information, lead us there quickly.

Would you like to meet your angel?

Angel Meditation

Sit quietly in a circle if participating in a group. Close your eyes and breathe deeply, letting your body relax. Think about moving higher and higher, protected in God's light. Imagine that you are moving up now above the clouds and into the world of angels, a beautiful world of soft, sweet musical tones and harmonies.

Ask your angel to come into your awareness, into your mind's eye where you can see or hear him/her. You will know when your angel is near from the love, peace and feeling of protection you will sense around you. You might see or sense a soft pink or golden light or some other soft color which says, "I am here."

When you feel connected to your angel, ask for a name. Listen carefully. Angels sometimes have names very different from ours, such as Ra-El-An or Arian-Na, or names like our own, such as Sara or Paul. Make special note of your angel's name and thank him/her for coming to visit. Send lots of love from your heart center. Anytime you want to contact your angel, simply ask.

There are special angels we can invite into our home to make our home environment more joyful, loving and beautiful, a happier place to live and be. It is very easy to create a space for your angel. Here is all you need to do:

Angel Exercise

It is important first to really want the angel to live in your home. Spend a few days thinking about the angel before asking him/her to come into your home to live.

Clean your house very thoroughly. Include the floors, walls and windows so that more light can come into your home. Your entire family can share in this experience. Angels like lots of light and love.

Light a white candle for the angel. White represents purity. Angels are light energies and will be drawn to the candlelight.

Sit quietly and focus your attention on the light of the candle. Close your eyes after a few moments and say out loud:

"Angel of the house, I thank you for being here. I wish my house to be filled with unconditional love – God's love. I ask that you live in my house and help make this house special, beautiful and as loving as I see that you are."

Sit quietly for a few moments. Feel the angel's presence. You will really enjoy having this special angel living in your home. Your home will be a house of love, joy and harmony.

HARMONY IN OUR ENVIRONMENT

The world (in general) and our environment (in particular) do not have to be filled with chaos, confusion and unhappiness. It is very simple to create harmony in any environment. Here are a few simple steps to follow:

- Play soft, angelic music rather than loud, irritating music. Soft, gentle sounds create harmony; irritating sounds create disharmony.
- Surround yourself with loving friends who support and allow you to be happy and joyful as you allow them to be happy and joyful. Sharing creates harmony. Laughing creates harmony.

- Share the chores at home as well as at school. Help others without expecting anything in return. Whatever you give out lovingly comes back to you ten times over. Working together creates harmony.
- Think positive, loving thoughts about yourself and others. Never judge or criticize yourself or anyone else. Seeing yourself as perfect and loving creates harmony in your life. As you create harmony in your own life, you create harmony in the lives of everyone who comes in contact with you.
- Meditate to center yourself, strengthening your connection to God as you do so. "Centering" yourself means to come into balance and harmony within yourself and with all parts of creation.

Centering Meditation

Breathe and relax your body and focus on your heart center. Imagine it filled with love from God and that it is the center not only of yourself but of the entire universe. Concentrate on this center until you feel it expand and come into balance.

"Grounding" your energies refers to making a firm connection to God and to the Earth, creating a balance between the universe and the Earth Mother.

Grounding Meditation

Imagine that your feet are tree roots that extend deep into the soil attaching you solidly to the Earth. Imagine that your body is the trunk of the tree, firm and tall. Your arms and head are the branches of the tree reaching up to God and the light. Feel your connection between God and the Earth. Feel the balance. Feel the harmony with all things.

- Come from your heart in all that you do, think or say. If an angry or negative thought comes to your mind, release it immediately, transmute it into pure love and light and replace it with positive, loving thoughts. Positive, loving thoughts create harmony.
- Release all fear and replace it with a sense of knowing that God is with you at all times and will always help you with any concern you may have. All fear is dissolved in God's light. Absence of fear and negative thoughts, feelings and emotions is harmony.
- Take a walk out in nature. Sit under a tree and absorb the sunshine and the colors, sounds and smells of nature. Nature is very soothing and balancing. The sound of water moving over stones in a creek can, for example, bring us quickly into harmony within ourselves and our environment even when we are feeling very sad.
- Release all attachment to material possessions. Realize that everything here on Earth is for you to borrow for the time you are here. You cannot take it with you when you travel back to God when your life experience is complete. Live simply and comfortably. As you release your connection to the material world, you find harmony.
- Do your part to love and protect the Earth. Recycle. Love the devic kingdom, the angelic kingdom and all the kingdoms on Earth. Pick up waste and encourage your friends and family to do the same. Help conserve the natural resources and honor all kingdoms as living beings that share the Earth experience. Each of us has come from the same Source. This is important to remember always.

AFFIRMATION: I see all things upon the Earth as equal, one family. I now create my world based on peace, harmony, joy, love, health and abundance. In so doing I help create harmony among creation.

9 • THE LAW OF TRANSMUTATION

The darkness of night consumes the light of day. The Sun sets in one portion of the world while rising in another. Although it is night, millions of stars and the beautiful silvery Moon dot the sky like tiny Christmas tree lights with one great star on top. Night is a time for rest, a time to dream and learn on the spiritual plane as we travel in our energy body from one dimension to another. It is during this time of rest that we prepare for the next day's experiences. Night is an important time for our spiritual growth because many of us are too busy during the day's activities to listen to our spiritual lessons.

Nighttime can bring to some individuals a feeling of fear. This fear exists for those who feel they cannot see with their physical eyes as well as in the light of day. To eliminate the fear of darkness (or any fear, for that matter), we simply turn on a light.

As the darkness disappears into light, so do our fears. In the light we can see what is in our space. We feel safe, secure and strong.

The Earth was created according to God's divine blueprint, which included positive energies of love, balance, harmony, peace, joy, happiness, health and abundance. All thought forms at the time of creation were of these positive qualities.

As we look around the Earth today, we find energies that are anything but those God created. Our world is experiencing war, crime, confusion, chaos, disease, disharmony, greed and the destruction of our natural resources. Sometimes it feels as though no one cares or that no one seems able to correct this picture.

The negative energies experienced on Earth at this time have been created not by God but by mankind in their misuse of free will. There are people who believe they are better than and more powerful than others, and who attempt to control and manipulate other people through various means for their own personal gain and benefit. There are those who feel they never have enough for themselves and through greed and selfishness attempt to take as much for themselves as possible, even at the expense of those they love and those they share the Earth experience with.

On an individual basis, at this time we as children of God are examining our belief systems. We are beginning to wade through old schools of thought, breaking down old structures, examining old programs, beliefs and ideas presented to us down through the generations. If we examine our world closely, we find that the governments, religions and education of today still reflect the past. We must remember that we cannot change what was. However, we can change our future and the future of the Earth by creating in this moment, together, a society based on love.

Change begins with each of us. We cannot change other people, because each of us has free will, the opportunity to decide for ourselves what is best. We tend to do what we want, what makes us happy, often without thinking of the consequences, about how our actions might affect others. As we begin to change our way of thinking, acting and believing, we set examples for others to follow. Change is a law of the universe. Change occurs at a constant pace, ever moving forward. To struggle against change creates obstacles and limitations. To move forward with change creates growth and happiness in our lives.

The Law of Transmutation states that the stronger, more prevalent energy in any situation will always win out. Thus if we allow feelings of sadness, anger, depression, fear, lack of self-esteem or self-worth, lack of faith, greed, self-centeredness and the like to dominate our thinking habits, we add to the negative energies that surround our Earth. If we allow such negative energies to dominate us and our society, we are not applying the Law of Transmutation as God intended.

This important universal law indicates that all darkness is consumed in light, meaning that any negative energy, thought form, feeling, and so on can be changed, or transmuted, into positive energy through God's Loving light, a light which is ever a part of us. We are never separate from this light even if we feel we are. It is important to learn how to use this light effectively to best understand the Law of Transmutation.

As each of us begins to recognize old patterns and thought forms that we are still carrying around with us like old garbage that no longer serves us, we begin to seek ways in which to release these old energies and bring in a new, more God-oriented way of being, thinking and feeling. It is important to remember that as old thought forms and negative energies are released, we take the responsibility for transmuting these energies rather than leave them for someone else to clean up or allow them to accumulate around the Earth. Can you imagine yourself feeling happy and joyful and having a lot of fun, and then suddenly walking into a wall of someone else's anger, fear or grief that they did not transmute?

Imagine a thought as a cloud or ball of energy. When you focus on releasing a thought or feeling, you visualize the thought and send it from your energy field out into the universe. Where does it go?

If the thought or feeling is simply released without concern for where it is going, it simply accumulates in the environment and adds to the band of negative thought forms around the Earth. It moves out from the Earth into the universe, affecting all of God's creations, affecting the balance and harmony of the universe. The band of negative thought forms around the Earth grows thicker and thicker each day. Every thought that is released from our minds affects this band, all living things, the Earth. Every negative thought form creates more unhappiness, imbalance, disharmony and disease for each of us to live with.

Imagine you are a "cosmic janitor" zooming around the universe, sweeping up all the unloving thought forms. You put them into a huge garbage container and close the lid, but very soon you find the container overflowing. What do you do? Negative thought forms are escaping all over the place. Now what?

We could all stop thinking negative thoughts. That would be wonderful. But until all humans awaken to their own divine perfection and begin to share, to experience and express unconditional love in all situations and with all people and all of creation, there will be a job for the cosmic janitor.

Those individuals who are now waking up from their long sleep and changing their ways of thinking and being are certainly assisting us in our cleanup task. There are still, however, those individuals who, through personal choice or lack of understanding, are unable to clean up their acts.

So we clean and clean, but there are more and more thoughts to clean up. This cycle has existed on the Earth for thousands of years. Over time the negative energy and its effects have increased in severity. We are each here on Earth to help change or transmute the negative energy to positive, loving energy. We are each here to assist in creating once again Heaven on Earth as it was at the time of creation.

The Law of Transmutation steps in to save the day. We can transmute or change the energy before it continues to damage our Earth and our own well-being. One might ask, "How can we transmute these thoughts?"

Thoughts are energy. All energy is in a constant state of motion. All energy can be changed from one form to another as demonstrated in the example of the ice cube experiment in the first chapter. To change an energy from one form to another, we simply change the thought that created the energy we wish to change.

We created a thought within our mind. We can just as easily change that thought by bringing into our mind a new form of energy. The Law of Transmutation tells us the stronger, most prevalent energy will always win out. If we keep thinking we are angry, for example, and the angry energy is allowed to keep building, it will feel more difficult to bring in the energy of love. *Whatever we give energy to with our thoughts, we create.*

If we feel anger and immediately replace the anger with loving thoughts of forgiveness, the angry energy cannot grow any stronger. The loving energy begins to move in, covering the anger like a thick blanket until all there is, is the loving energy. The more love we focus on, the more love we create and the more love we feel and express.

Many times during the day, thoughts and feelings enter our conscious mind that do not make us feel good about ourselves or others. Where do these thoughts and feelings come from? We must realize that since all is energy, we live in a sea of energy created by everyone and everything and we are affected by our environment, which is energy. We can walk into a crowd of people feeling very happy. If the general expression of energy from the crowd is happiness, we will maintain our own happiness. However, if there is unhappy energy present and we allow that energy to affect us, we become unhappy. The energy of unhappiness is now a part of us.

Change begins with each of us. Thus as we begin to transmute or change negative thoughts, we affect others. Our energy affects all those living things we come in contact with. If we are feeling unhappy, and we send out unhappy energy from our auric field and other people can begin to feel unhappy, too. Plants and animals that experience our unhappy energy will not be as healthy and happy.

As we stay balanced within ourselves and maintain a happy feeling inside, that feeling will be reflected on the outside; everyone and everything that comes in contact with our happy energy will be affected in a positive way.

Exercise

For this exercise you will need a large magnet and some nails, screws, tacks, paper clips, or other such metal objects.

Let each metal object represent some form of negative thought. For example, the nail can represent anger; the screw, grief; the tack, competition; the paper clip, greed; and so forth. Place the metal objects on a table top and hold the magnet out to draw the objects to it.

You are the magnet. Your electromagnetic field, which surrounds your body, acts like a magnet, drawing thoughts, feelings and emotions to you from the outside world.

Whatever we think about or focus on is drawn into and stored in our energy field, the aura, which vibrates as pure energy. The aura sends impulses in the form of electrical current into the universe. Like the magnet in the above exercise, these thoughts bring into our lives just what we have been thinking and believing as our truth. Whether positive or negative, we attract people and situations into our lives to help us recognize those areas of thinking and feeling we need to bring back into balance.

Through our ability to recognize those areas of our thinking, feeling and communication processes that are not coming from a God-space, we are able to change those patterns through positive thinking, through affirmations or positive statements and by not allowing anything but positive feelings to remain in our being. We then change our own life experiences and situations, and influence positively the world around us.

Now, for each negative thought you have attached to the metal objects in the above exercise, think of the positive opposite. For example, change anger to happiness, grief to joy, competition to sharing, greed to unity. Again, you are the magnet. Draw these positive qualities/thoughts to yourself. How do you feel?

To determine how our thoughts, feelings and words may be affecting ourselves, other people and the world around us, we must first examine ourselves. How do we see ourselves and other people? How do we relate to our families and friends? How do we view our school experiences, our community, the Earth? The following meditation allows each of us to reflect on that part of our lives where we may be creating negative experiences. As we become aware of the areas needing change, we can better transmute the energy that no longer serves us.

Meditation to Change Your World

Sit in a comfortable position with your spine straight to allow the energy to flow freely. Take a few deep breaths, relaxing your body more and more as you breathe. Allow your conscious mind to flow into a peaceful connection to the place within yourself where you connect with God. Feel the strength, the power, love, joy and happiness that comes to you as you connect with God.

Imagine you are standing in front of a large mirror. The mirror reflects back to you images that relate to different aspects of your life experiences here on Earth. Pay close attention to how you might create a more perfect life experience for yourself and a more perfect world by changing your thought processes regarding the different areas of your life, which we will explore in this meditation.

*First, look at **your body**. Begin with the top of your head and slowly let your eyes move downward, examining every aspect of yourself. How do you feel about your body? Are you happy with what you see? Do you have any thoughts about yourself that might be creating disharmony in your life? Is your hair the wrong color, your nose too large or too small? Are you too fat, too thin? Are you too tall or too short?*

Now visualize yourself as perfect in every way, a reflection of God. "I am a beautiful, happy, loving person. I am perfect in every way. I am a part of God and God is a part of me. I love myself and accept myself just as I am, for if I am made in the image of God and God is perfect, I must be perfect also."

***Your family** members are now reflected in the mirror. How do you see your relationship to your mother, father, brothers, sisters and other relatives? Do you feel loved, accepted, respected? Or do you feel left out, rejected, different? Are you able to communicate openly with your family members, or do you feel they will never understand and accept you? Do you feel that one family member is loved more than you or given more attention than you, or is everyone treated equally?*

Imagine having the perfect family relationship, like one large circle where each gives and receives from the others equally. Feel the love flowing in your family unit. See your family as you would like them to be. "I give and receive equally in my family unit. We are happy, joyful and loving. God is the center of our family unit, and through our oneness with God and each other, we find joy and peace."

*Visualize **your friends**. Do your friends treat you as you would like to be treated? Do you have friends who are angry? Are you angry? Do your friends include you in their activities, or do you feel left out? Do they tease you, make fun of you, or you of them?*

Now create beautiful, loving friendships. See all your friends happy, loving and joyful, sharing their experiences with you equally. See your friends treating you as you would like to be treated and you treating your friends in a like manner. Remember, the more love you feel within yourself, the more love you express outward, the happier and more joyful your thoughts, conversations, feelings and actions, then the more loving and joyful friendships you will bring into your life experience. "I experience loving and joyful relationships with my friends. I am accepted just as I am and I accept them just as they are. We are each perfect in every way."

*How do you see **your school** experience? Do you see school as a burden, a place where you are forced to participate and wish you did not have to go? Or is school a wonderful place to connect with others and to participate in a learning and growing situation? Do you enjoy your studies, or do you find them a burden?*

See school as a place of learning, sharing and growing. Everything comes to you easily and effortlessly — good grades, time to study, friendships, activities, great teachers. Imagine school as a place of sharing and exchanging ideas and experiences with new friends. See school as a bridge in the process of maturing and venturing out into the world as a whole, complete and prepared individual. "I do well in school. School is a wonderful place of learning and growing. I have plenty of time to study. I make good grades and I am proud of the work I accomplish."

*As you examine **your neighborhood**, how do you feel? Are there things within your neighborhood or community you would like to change? Are there sufficient places for young people to go to have a good time? Are there parts of your community where people are suffering and you would like to see some changes made to help them? Are there certain rules and regulations you have experienced in your community that seem unfair or outdated?*

Imagine your community as perfect in every way, everyone sharing and caring about one another. See the community just as you would like it to be and with you as a caring participant. Feel the happiness, joy, the love within your community. "I create a loving and joyful environment, because I am loving and joyful within myself. I express this love and joy in all that I do, think and say."

*Now take a good look at **the world** around you. What do you see? What are some of the things that make you unhappy? What are some of the things you are happy with? What would you like to change? Do you see poverty, illness, crime, angry and fearful people? Or do you see happy, joyful, loving people, always expressing God in all that they do? How can you change what you do not like?*

Change begins with you. Radiate from your heart all the God-love that you are. Send this love out into the world and imagine that as this God-love touches all parts of the Earth that need healing, the love changes everything negative to something positive and loving. Now imagine the world just as you would like to see it. "All is perfect in my world. The entire Earth is bathed in divine love."

Focus your attention on what you have just created within and outside of yourself, in your family unit, your school, community, the Earth. See your environment just as you want it to be. Focus all the love from within your heart on this image. Open your eyes when you feel ready.

How did you feel about the changes you made in this meditation? Do you feel you can change whatever you focus on?

In this meditation we used positive statements called *affirmations* to support the positive change we were creating. Affirmations are very powerful statements that can, in fact, bring about rapid change. Affirmations help us focus our thoughts and feelings in a positive way. Positive thoughts create positive results.

To begin to make changes in our life experiences, we must each be aware of the negative thoughts we personally are holding onto. The following list presents some of the more common negative thoughts and emotions that we as human beings bring into our life experiences. Perhaps you can think of others and add them to the list.

Fear: "I'm afraid."
Anger: "I'm furious."
Sadness: "I'm unhappy."
Guilt: "I regret doing that."
Shame: "I feel ashamed of myself."
Selfishness: "That's mine!"
Unlovability: "No one loves me."
Unworthiness: "I am not worth anything."
Unhappiness: "There's nothing good in the world."
Worry/concern: "What if this or that happens?"
Competition: "I have to be better than him/her."
Distrust/withholding: "I don't want you to take advantage of me."
Lack of self-confidence: "I can't do anything right."
Fear of failure: "What if I don't succeed?"

Despair/depression: "What's the use?"
Feeling lack: "I don't have enough."
Neediness: "I need . . ."
Self-criticism: "I'm not pretty/handsome."
Self-judgment: "No one likes me because I'm not like them."
Apathy/loss of interest: "I just don't care about anything."
Focus on past: "If I could only do that over again" or "I can't forgive what they did to me."
Limited thinking: "I can do this only if you help me."
Undeserving: "I don't deserve nice things."
Fear of obstacles: "I can't because . . ."

Choose those items from the above list that you feel are thoughts or feelings you have been experiencing, or create your own. List them on a piece of paper. On another piece of paper, write down the positive aspects of the negative thoughts. For example, "I'm afraid of the dark" can be changed to "I am protected in God's love and light. I am safe."

Instead of "I can do this only if you help me," write "I can do anything I choose to do." "I don't have enough" is changed to "I have an abundance of everything to create for me happiness and comfort."

Love is the most powerful vibration in God's universe. Love can change any negative energy to positive energy quickly and easily. Focus on bringing God-love into your heart and your entire body. Send love to your fears, anger, sadness and so on. The love will fill your whole body and mind with lightness and a soft feeling, with a sense of comfort and peace. Love changes or transmutes negative thought forms to positive waves of love.

There are other tools of transmutation we can use to clean up our negative thought forms before they can do any damage in affecting others or the Earth. In working with these tools, we can change all unwanted energy simply by visualizing it changed into pure love and light. As a cosmic janitor with some new tools, now we can really clean up after ourselves and reduce the negative energy around the Earth and within our entire universe.

THE VIOLET FLAME

There is a very special ascended master who works very closely with each of us when we learn how to apply this law. His name is St. Germaine. He does not have a physical form as we do, yet he is very much concerned with our spiritual growth and happiness.

St. Germaine loves the Earth and all the beings living on the Earth. Because of this great love and the concern he has for bringing peace and love, balance and harmony back to the Earth, he went before the great karmic board in the heavens and asked permission to bring God's transmuting Violet Flame to Earth in a last great attempt to help people and the Earth evolve spiritually. The flame had been used before, but people had abused its power. Promising to guard the use of the flame personally, St. Germaine was granted his request.

Because God loves all of us so much, He/She wanted us to have all the possible chances to change the negative energies we have created on Earth. God has given us many tools and much encouragement in our spiritual evolution. God does not punish us, but allows us to learn through what we choose to experience.

Thus God lovingly gives to us this Violet Flame and lessons in its appropriate use as a tool of transmutation. The Violet Flame is the heart flame of God and appears violet when we see it in our mind's eye. The flame's purpose is to purify and transmute into love and light all the negative thoughts, feelings and emotions released by anyone on the Earth. From God all living things came, and to God all things return, including all energy released, both negative and positive. Because God is love, His/Her love transmutes all negative energy immediately into love and light. No negative thought form from mankind can ever affect God.

The transmuting Violet Flame does not harm, burn or cause pain, but is a powerful tool of change. As we work with it we might feel nothing but a lightness in our body and mind, as though something has been lifted from our energy field.

Negative energy is dense and heavy. Positive energy is light and happy. Thus when you feel lighter, you will know that you have transmuted more of the old negative energy.

Violet Flame Exercise

Stand straight and tall, arms at your sides. Take a few deep breaths to relax your body. Ask Master St. Germaine to come forward and help you build the beautiful Violet Flame. Imagine this flame all around you. You are standing in the middle of the flame. You can feel or sense its coldness, its power, its love.

Let any unhappy or negative thought, emotion or feeling come into your mind. Focus your attention on one thought at a time. Ask this thought to be consumed in the Violet Flame. Acknowledge and thank this feeling or emotion for being there, but tell it now that it is time for it to leave, that it no longer serves you in any way.

Visualize this thought, feeling or emotion being dissolved in the Violet Flame and changing back into pure light-love energy, back into the heart of God.

You can do this exercise any time you feel or think about something negative, a thought you do not want in your mind. Any thought that is not loving and kind is not a thought you want to hold onto. Dissolve it immediately in the Violet Flame and you will be free from having to continue feeling the energy.

THE CRYSTAL SPIRAL

The Crystal Spiral is another tool by which we can release and transmute old patterns and thought forms that we no longer wish to keep.

Exercise

Sit quietly, spine straight, and begin to take some long, deep breaths. Feel a clear flame energy in your heart, a crystal-clear flame. Feel the flame. You do not have to see it.

Imagine the flame inside a tube that is in the center of your heart. Now imagine the flame as two spirals – one moving clockwise, the other counterclockwise. The spirals resemble two bedsprings (or Slinkies) that are inside each other, but spin in two different directions.

The spirals of crystal-clear liquid-light energy in the tube move up and down at the same time. Feel the spiral going both into the Earth and all the way up to God.

Feeling yourself in the spiral energy, connect with God's love. Stay in that very high feeling space. Move your attention higher and higher until you can feel God all around you, until you are in that place of knowing.

Ask an emotion or thought you wish to release to come into your awareness. For example: "I don't have any friends." In looking at this feeling/thought, you might begin to see or feel a picture in your higher mind, your place of knowing, that place where we each simply know things without questioning where it comes from. In a moment you realize you have tried to make your friends do what you wanted. You feel you have not been willing to allow them to choose things. You have been trying to control everyone and everything. You begin to clearly see the picture that if you were more willing to share in things your friends wanted to do, you might be included more often.

Now you have an opportunity to change the energy. First, forgive yourself for creating this lesson in sharing. We are all here on Earth to learn lessons. Lessons may repeat themselves over and over until we learn them; then we move on to something new. Thank the lesson for making itself known to you. Release the energy into the spiral. "Thank you, energy, for helping me learn this lesson about sharing. I forgive myself for holding onto this lesson, but you are no longer useful for me. I have learned you well. I now release you into the spiral. I am free."

Imagine this energy moving into the white liquid-light spiral and up into God. Once more the energy has returned to God to be re-created into something else. Through the spiral you have transmuted the unwanted energy. The spiral is available to each of us at any time to transmute any situation, feeling, thought or emotion.

TRANSMUTING ILLNESS TO WELLNESS

Whatever we give energy to, whatever we think about — we create. If we focus on our divine perfection, we create it in all ways in our physical, emotional, mental and spiritual bodies. We create this sense of perfection in our environment, and this energy affects those who come in contact with it. As we visualize ourselves as perfect, we create perfection. Nothing outside of perfection exists within or outside of us.

On the other hand, if we think about anything other than perfection, we create imbalance, disharmony and disease in our bodies and our environment. Let's say we have a fever and stomachache. We visit the doctor, who tells us we have the stomach flu. We acknowledge, "Okay, I have the flu." The doctor might give us a prescription or tell us to go home and get plenty of rest.

The visit to the doctor has reinforced the thought that there is something wrong with our body: we have "the flu." The prescription also reinforces the idea that there is something out of balance. It is important to realize that all disease as we know it begins with a thought; something we hear or feel about ourselves or something we fear we might catch, becomes our truth. We create it in our body as illness.

Suppose we feel that something is out of balance in our body. We feel feverish and our stomach seems to be a bit upset. With this awareness that something is out of balance in our body comes the need to examine the thought that created the symptoms. The physical body reacts like this only when we have not paid attention to all the warnings expressed in our mental (thinking) body and our emotional (feeling) body.

Anytime we feel out of balance, we can sit or lie down and create the white-light spiral. Ask the thought that created the imbalance to come into our awareness. Perhaps we need more rest or we need to complete one project before starting another. Perhaps we need more meditation time to strengthen our connection with God. Perhaps there is a fear about something we do not want to deal with at school or about having to face someone who is angry at us. We also need to ask the question, "Have I accepted what someone else says is wrong with me?"

Your mother says, "The flu is going around. Don't get too close to anyone you feel might be coming down with the flu. The flu makes you very sick. You will have to stay in bed instead of going outside and playing with your friends." The seed thought has been planted. We heard our mother warn us about the possibility of catching the flu from a friend. After hearing these words giving them thought, fearing the flu, we sit next to a friend at school who feels feverish, a bit tired. We might jump to the conclusion that the person has the flu and think, "Now I am going to have the flu also." By attaching the experience at school to Mother's words, the flu symptoms can develop. If the energy surrounding the fear of catching the flu is released immediately, however, and transmuted into love and light in the spiral, the symptoms disappear and we stay healthy and balanced.

In the world today, we are dealing with health concerns of cancer, AIDS, heart disease, diabetes — each of which is created from a fear, thought or belief in the mental body of an individual. Cancer and AIDS seem to have gotten out of hand. Although medical practitioners have found ways to ease the symptoms and sometimes "cure" the illness, these two diseases still seem to be in control.

People today have great fear of catching either of these two diseases. AIDS is said to be highly contagious and we are warned not to get involved with people displaying this disease. AIDS comes from the thought form of hating ourselves or of self-destruction ("I don't want to be here, so I will create something so I can go back to God.") Cancer can occur in any part of the body and is also a reflection of anger held in the body until the anger begins to eat away at the body. In either case, as the anger or self-hate or other negative emotions are released, the body can then heal itself and release the disease with the thought that created it.

As we read material concerning such disease, as we listen to other people's fears, we can become more and more concerned for our own well-being. Remember: whatever we focus our attention on is drawn to us. If we do not focus on or fear a disease, we will not bring it into our experience. Release the fear or concern; release the need for such a lesson.

We each have the power to create whatever we wish to experience in this life. We can choose positive experiences or negative ones simply by expressing thoughts and feelings within our being. To effectively work with the Law of Transmutation, it is important to slow down our life processes, to "think before we think," to focus on the positive and immediately use our tools to transmute all energy that no longer serves us.

TRANSMUTING NEGATIVE THOUGHT FORMS SURROUNDING THE EARTH

Over the eons of time that mankind has lived on planet Earth, moving further and further from oneness with God, becoming more and more separate from all of creation, we have focused on confusion, chaos, war, destruction, greed, judgment, discrimination, power struggles and control. At the same time, mankind has continued to deplete the natural resources of this great planet. The negative energy mankind has continued to visit upon the Earth has formed what we call the *astral belt*.

This belt has grown in density and intensity with each negative experience and expression released. Because this band is always there, we often feel sad or depressed and do not fully understand why. Many times we must ask ourselves, is this my sadness, or someone else's? Where is it coming from?

We do not have to sit on the sidelines and watch the destruction of the Earth and our own happiness. We can transmute these thoughts with the tools we have been given, according to the Law of Transmutation: the more powerful energy always wins. Everything in the universe is subject to change, and we are each responsible for our own thoughts and actions. Thus, as we clean up our own thoughts, we help the Earth. As we send healing to our planet, we help the Earth and all her living things. As we focus on positive, loving energy, the negative energy is transmuted, changed. The astral belt can then begin to dissolve in light.

Two Earth Healing Meditations

Sit quietly. Visualize the Earth. Around the Earth you can see gray clouds of negative thought forms from other people. These thought forms are anger, hate, confusion, fear, pain, suffering, doubt, guilt, shame and more.

Imagine a picture in your mind's eye of God's Violet Flame. Place the Earth in the center of the flame. Visualize it transmuting all the negative thoughts around the Earth into pure light and love. The negative energy travels back to the heart of God, where it returns to love energy.

From your heart send love to the Earth. Imagine the Earth being cleansed and healed, all parts of her being freed of pollution and the abuse of people. See waves of love surround the Earth. See the Earth smile.

If you wish you may focus each meditation on a particular group of people or on one area of concern for the Earth, such as the rainforests, areas of war and conflict such as the Middle East and so on. See the Violet Flame change people's attitudes about the importance of the rainforests. See people respect the rainforests and care for them. See all areas of war being replaced with the energy of love and peace. The more you work with this meditation, the lighter and brighter the Earth will feel.

❋　　❋　　❋　　❋

Sit quietly and visualize the Earth in your mind's eye. In the center of the Earth imagine a crystal-clear flame of light and place the flame inside a tube that runs through the center of the Earth. Inside the tube imagine two spirals of crystal-clear liquid light, one spiral moving clockwise and the other moving counterclockwise.

The spirals move up and down and in and out. Imagine all the negative energy on the Earth, around the Earth and in the atmosphere being placed into the spirals and transmuted into love and light. See the spirals cleanse and heal the Earth. The Earth is fresh and new.

The Law of Transmutation protects the entire universe and all of creation. Always remember that we are not helpless victims of what we have helped create through our separation from God's love, light and laws. As we think and feel things that are not positive, we can immediately create in our mind the Violet Flame or the crystal liquid-light spirals and change the unwanted energy to loving, positive energy. Positive thoughts create positive life experiences. Positive life experiences are filled with love, joy, and loving friends.

AFFIRMATION: I am a powerful part of God, capable of changing all unwanted thoughts, feelings and emotions into pure love and light. As I transmute unwanted energies, I create love and light within myself. I express this love and light outwardly with other people, all living things, with the Earth and God's universe. The love I express is returned to me. I am love. I am loved.

10 • THE LAW OF BALANCE

In Chapter Four we discussed the Law of Polarity. This law showed us how God created everything within this universe to be in balance, and through this balance the universe was able to exist. The law points out to us that where there is no balance, there can be no harmony. Balance and harmony go hand in hand.

What happens when we are too hot or too cold, when we eat too much or not enough? What happens when we feel unhappy all the time; when we are always happy, no matter what life brings to us to deal with?

Balance is very important to the universe, our Earth, to all living things. If we watch a performer balancing on a tightrope, what happens if he leans too much to one side or the other? If he stays in the center, he is able to balance on the wire and perform.

We find it necessary to create balance in our diet. If we eat too many sweets, for instance, we may create a stomachache. When we eat foods that are good for us, foods that provide necessary vitamins and minerals that give us the energy we need each day, we feel strong and healthy. Our bodies are in balance. If we eat foods that are not good for us or do not provide the necessary nutrients, our bodies might feel tired and weak, unable to perform even the simplest task. We might even begin to feel sick.

What are some of the areas in our daily lives where we need to create balance?

1. Sleep (or rest)

2. Diet (food)

3. Water and juices

4. Exercise and play

5. Emotions, positive or negative

6. Thoughts, positive or negative

7. Physical and spiritual ideals

Can you list others?

When we are in balance, we are better able to find the center of our God presence within, which helps us align with the physical and spiritual worlds. When we are in balance, we can better listen to our intuition, through which we hear, feel and know God. Being in balance means to not let anyone or anything change the way we feel about something. It means to hold to our truth, following what we know inside to be right for us, believing in ourselves and knowing we have value.

Being in balance means to listen to your own feelings and act on what is right for you in the present moment.

You have a friend at school who wants you to help her cheat on her homework. You do not want to help her cheat because you feel it is wrong. Your friend says she will not be your friend ever again if you do not help her. What do you do?

If you help her cheat, you will be doing something that does not feel right to you. It makes you feel uncomfortable and guilty. If you help her, you are giving your power to her. If you do not help her, you might lose her as a friend, but you will keep your personal power.

Also, if you are honest, you will attract or bring into your life honest people. This person might not want to be your friend any longer, but you will be happier and enjoy even more the new friendships you will create.

Have you ever had a friend like this, one who wanted you to do something you knew was wrong, but you did it anyway just to keep the friendship? Were you afraid you would not have any friends if you refused to do what the friend suggested? What happened?

Have you ever tried to make one of your friends do something he/she did not want to do?

If so, you were trying to take their power away. What happened?

Know when to pay attention to your own feelings and needs, and when to be selfless – to understand the effect your actions have on others. Then choose the appropriate action and take it.

Your friend is constantly teasing and making fun of you. You like this friend, but you don't like to be teased. How can you deal with this person?

You can become angry and tell the friend to stop or you won't be her friend any longer.

You can tease her and probably make her angry at you as well.

You can lovingly ask her to stop, explaining how it makes you feel.

Now put yourself in each of these pictures. How would each situation make you feel inside? What should you do?

Do not feel responsible for other people's happiness. Each of us creates his or her own happiness. We are each 100% responsible only for ourselves.

You give away your power when you let others get the best of you. If you lovingly settle your problems, you keep your power and your friends as well.

Your friend is very unhappy whenever you are playing with others. He thinks you should play only with him. How would you deal with this friend?

Send love to your friend. Continue to play with other children. Encourage your friend to join in the fun. Help him feel part of the larger whole and that everyone in the group accepts and includes him.

Give to others what you yourself want to receive – love, support, appreciation, acknowledgment. As you give from your heart, you will receive the same in return.

You want to have your classmates support you in winning the position of class president. How can you gain their support?

What you give out you get back. If you offer your support to your classmates, helping them with their election campaigns, they will, help you in turn.

Turn and look right at the fear. Your fear will dissolve in light as you shine God's love at the fear.

We give our power away by being afraid. Is there something you have been afraid of lately?

Fear is a feeling of heaviness, worry, concern. It is a feeling that separates us from God's love and light existing within each of us. Fear is a feeling that keeps us from listening to God's voice when we ask for help. Fear is merely an absence of light.

To get rid of fear, sit in a chair with your spine very straight, feet flat on the floor. Rest your hands on your thighs. Breathe deeply and let your body relax. Imagine something or someone you fear. See this situation or person clearly in your imagination. Now imagine God's light coming down through the top of your head, out through your Heart Chakra and aimed right at the fear. See the fear dissolve in the light. The fear is gone. Wasn't that easy?

Love and accept who you are, not who you will be or should be. Know you are perfect just as you are.

Your personal power comes from loving yourself for who you are right now, not for who you want to be. Many of us try to be someone we cannot be. We try to be what someone else wants us to be. If we try to be what we cannot be, what someone else wants us to be, we are giving our personal power away.

The best way to know yourself, to know your own power, is to sit quietly alone, away from other people who might interrupt you. Let your mind be quiet. Let all thoughts flow like a breeze right out of your head. Go inside. Be one with your Higher Self, one with God. Let's try a special meditation.

Love Meditation

Sit quietly. Breathe deeply, allowing your body to relax more and more with each breath, in and out. Listen to the soft music, to your heartbeat. Listen to your breathing. Concentrate on that special place within yourself, that place where you feel love. Be in that loving space now.

Let the love expand . . . love for all things everywhere. Love for God, for all the people of the world, for all the plants, trees and animals, for all the rocks. Let the love expand . . . expand . . . expand. Best of all, let that love flow into you and all around you, into all things in your environment, into the entire Earth and all living things. **Love yourself first.**

CREATING BALANCE IN THE FOUR BODIES

Change begins with one person. If we are out of balance, we help create imbalance in the world and the universe.

To be in perfect balance, we must bring all four bodies into balance. Let's make a chart. What things can you see in yourself that are creating an imbalance in each of the four bodies listed below?

Physical Body

The physical body senses the outside world with the five senses of sight, hearing, feeling, tasting and smelling. It thinks with the conscious mind and works from a place of personal ego, the self — me. In examining the physical body, we must look at each body part to determine where we think something is not in balance. Do we need to wear glasses, use a hearing aid, walk with a cane? Do we have problems with smelling or tasting things? Are we sick a lot? Do we eat right? Do we get enough rest? List below those things you see in yourself that are not in balance in your physical body.

_____ _____

_____ _____

Emotional Body

The emotional body deals with our feelings. Are we angry, sad, happy, joyful, ashamed, feeling guilty about something, feeling unworthy, lacking in self-confidence? Do we feel oversensitive when people speak to us? Are we overemotional, crying a great deal or reacting in some other way that is not acceptable to others?

In what way do you feel your emotional body is out of balance, and why do you feel it is affected this way?

_____ _____

_____ _____

Mental Body

The mental body deals with our thoughts. It is in the mental body that disease first makes its presence known. We might think we are not wanted or accepted, that we are not good enough, that we don't do anything right. We might think we are special and loved, that we have important work to do here and perhaps no one else agrees with us and that makes us feel wrong.

Examine your thoughts. How do you think about yourself and who you are? How do you think your thoughts may be affecting your life?

_____ _____

_____ _____

Spiritual Body

The spiritual body, our Higher Self, is always connected to God and exists in an energy of total love and acceptance. Sometimes we do not feel connected to God. Sometimes we feel as though we have done something God does not approve of. Sometimes we wonder whether or not God really exists, and if so, how can we know that to be true?

Look at your relationship to God. How do you feel about God? Do you feel love of a high level coming into your heart? Do you express this love openly to all living things? Do you feel God loves and accepts you no matter what you do, whether you feel it is right or wrong? List your feelings on the following lines.

_____   _____

_____   _____

Meditation

The following meditation will help bring all your bodies into balance and oneness with God.

Close your eyes. Breathe deeply. Relax your body from the tips of your toes to the top of your head. Focus on a bright blue light in the center of your forehead. Let this light help you feel relaxed and calm.

Imagine your physical body standing straight and tall. See yourself happy, healthy and calm. Both feet are flat on the floor. Your arms are at your side in a comfortable position. Breathe deeply. Breathe in loving pink light. Breathe out any pain, sore spots or stuck feelings in your body. Imagine these spots as clouds of gray energy leaving your body as you breathe out. As these clouds leave your body, see them fade into pure, loving light.

Now, just outside your physical body is your energy body, the emotional body. This is the body containing many colors that reflect different emotions or feelings. Focus on the colors you are feeling in your energy body now. Is there any feeling that is uncomfortable? Do you feel sad or angry? Do you feel unloved, guilty, ashamed? Do you feel you are not as good as other family members or friends? What are you feeling?

Bring love from God as a pink light. Let this light fill your entire body with loving energy. As you breathe, draw in love. Breathe out any feelings you no longer want in your body. If the unwanted feeling does not wish to leave, send more and more love into that feeling until it fades into light.

Now imagine your mental body. What do you think about? Are you thinking happy, loving thoughts, or unhappy, angry thoughts? Let your mind open like a little door, allowing more and more light into your mind. Along with the light, let love flow into your mind. Let the love and light fill your mental body until there are no other thoughts – just loving, happy thoughts.

Imagine your spiritual body glowing brighter and brighter in white light until every part of your body is a reflection of the white light. Let the light grow larger and larger, brighter and brighter. See all your bodies inside this white light. Feel the loving energy of God all around you. Feel your connectedness to God, to the universe, to all of creation. Feel white light flowing like a number eight, from the Earth up through your heart and on up to God, then back down through your heart to the Earth.

Feel yourself balanced, in harmony with all things everywhere. See yourself as part of God and God as part of you. Open your eyes as you feel ready. Enjoy your new feeling of balance with all things.

AFFIRMATION: *I am special. I am one with all things of Creation. I accept responsibility for maintaining balance within myself, knowing that I am setting an example for all others. I am balance in all that I do.*

11 • THE LAW OF PERFECTION

God is a loving energy through which all things have been created. It is God's love that acts as the glue holding all His/Her creation together. Take away the love and what we see and experience would no longer exist. We cannot exist without God. We cannot exist without God's love for each of us.

Imagine God as a great golden light of energy radiating outward into All That Is. Imagine this golden light as warm, loving energy, the type of energy that makes you feel safe and secure, or the way you feel on a cold winter's night when you are tucked snugly in your warm bed.

Now imagine that you are a tiny spark of light, a part of this great golden light of God. In one sense, you can compare yourself to a tiny drop of water from a great ocean. Even though you have been separated from the ocean, you are still made up of all the same qualities, the same minerals, molecules and atoms as the larger body of water.

As in this example, each of us is but a tiny droplet of energy from God. Even though we have been separated from God in the sense of now having a physical body and living in a physical world, we are still energy and light — God's light and love. Within each of us is a blueprint a special coding that is the same as the blueprint of God. We never forget this special coding. It is ever a part of us. It is deep within each of us, and as we begin to evolve back closer and closer to God through spiritual learning and awakening processes, this coding becomes activated; it begins to help us remember who we truly are, one with God.

God is perfect. God does not have bad days. God does not get angry or sick. God does not stop loving us simply because we have done something we feel He/She disapproves of.

God is love. In love there is nothing that is in any way imperfect or negative. Anything outside of love — that is, anything that is not loving — cannot be part of God's perfection.

When God created us, He/She created each of us as perfect, just as God is perfect. When we think of something that we consider perfect, we usually think of something that is whole, balanced, beautiful, loving, without any blemishes or flaws.

We were each created to be perfect, whole, healthy, happy, joyful and prosperous beings. Only by our own free choice have we become otherwise. Through free will we can do anything we want. However, we must remember that whenever we do something that extends outside God's laws, we create challenges and imperfections along the way.

EXAMINING IMPERFECTION

To better understand perfection, let's examine what we feel are imperfections, or things outside of God's perfection. Let's look at our own concept or idea of what is or is not perfect.

Many times people are born in different states of what we perceive to be imperfection. For example, people are born blind, deaf, unable to speak, with one leg or arm deformed or shorter than the other or even totally absent. Through accidents, individuals can end up in a situation where they are unable to feed themselves or move their arms and legs. Burn victims often display serious scarring that can cause the individual embarrassment or feelings of rejection. We often see these individuals as imperfect.

Remember, each of these individuals was created in divine perfection. Even though in the physical body there are deformities or what appear to be imperfections, in the lightbody, the energy body, the Higher Self, there is perfection. When an organ is removed surgically, in the etheric body and all the lightbodies the organ is still present. When a person loses a hand, an arm, leg or foot, sometimes there is a sensation that the limb is still present. This "ghost limb" is the energy body still resonating or vibrating with the perfection in which it was created.

When the physical body does not appear perfect, it is often a lesson to the rest of us to look deeper and see that it is not what is on the outside that is important, but what is on the inside, in the heart. An individual with a physical deformity could be here to teach us not to judge and discriminate, but to love unconditionally from our hearts no matter what the physical appearance.

Remember: your lightbody, your soul, is always perfect. The physical body is only the shell that houses your energy body, that part of you always connected to God. No matter what you look like on the outside, on the inside is the light of God — divine perfection.

Exercise

Stand in front of a mirror and look at yourself closely. Take special note of anything that stands out about yourself. Write down anything you see or feel that is not in perfect harmony with the part of you that resonates from God's love and light. That is, in what ways do you feel you are not working from your loving God-space? Do you judge or discriminate against others or yourself? Do you criticize yourself or others? Do you abuse your physical body in some way — drugs, alcohol, unhealthy diet, not enough rest and so on?

As you look at your face, let your eyes relax. Keep focused on a point on your face until your face seems to disappear or change. You can often begin to see a light. That light is your soul's light. You are looking at that part of yourself that is always perfect. What you feel and see from this experience is divine love and perfection.

THOUGHTS CAN CREATE PERFECTION OR IMPERFECTION

From the energy of thought, God created the heavens and the Earth and all the living things we share space with in the universe. God's thought was put forth with clear intent, with love. God imagined what He/She wanted to create, and as He/She imagined it clearly and precisely, it became reality. Because God is perfect, all that God created is perfect, including mankind.

In life on Earth, by experiencing free will, we have taken upon ourselves to create imperfection. We have tried to control each other, to take from one another; we express greed and selfishness, which are certainly not God-qualities or qualities of perfection.

What we think, we create. This is one of God's universal laws. Thus if we are thinking loving thoughts, if we are thinking from our God-selves, we are thinking and creating in the form of perfection as God creates. If, however, we are thinking from our conscious minds and in terms of selfishness, greed, power, control and so on, we are creating imperfection.

Imperfect thoughts can create many types of imbalances in ourselves and in our world. Our thoughts can actually make us sick. We can fear cancer, for example, and our fear can bring it to us. We can think about how lonely we are and create even more loneliness. Or we can think of ourselves in a loving way, perfect, happy, healthy and whole, and that is what we will create.

Exercise

Sit quietly and let your body relax. Think about some situation occurring in your life at home or at school. How is the situation making you feel? How are you dealing with it?

For example, you feel angry inside. You don't know what this angry feeling is all about. Every time someone tries to encourage you to do something with them, you yell at them and walk away. Now no one wants to include you in their activities. You feel very lonely and abandoned.

Imagine one of these individuals coming to you to invite you to a play. The person asks if you would be one of the drivers for the evening. You feel suddenly you are being taken advantage of. You feel you are always the one driving to these events. Now you realize why you have been angry and why you have not been participating with your friends.

Tell this individual that you would love to accompany them to the play, but that you will be unable to drive this time. Feel your body full of love as you speak to the person. Stay in this very loving space. Bring love down from God through the top of your heart and out your heart center. Fill your heart with more and more love as you speak. Smile. Stand in your God-power and let the individual know how you feel. If the person does not accept your offer, you know this individual is only wanting to use you. However, if he/she says, "Of course, we'll ask Ann to drive this time," you will feel more accepted, loved and part of the group. Think love. Think of what you want to create in a loving way, and that is what you will create. The perfect situation will occur.

ILLNESS AS IMPERFECTION

Within each of us is a divine blueprint known as the *immaculate concept*, that part of us which is an exact duplicate copy of God's perfection. This concept is held within each of us, and when we connect to our Higher Self, our God-self, we are able to clearly see this divine blueprint in all life and in ourselves.

Illness is not God-reality. Illness is an illusion we create through imperfect thinking. Anytime we are not feeling well, we need to sit quietly, breathe deeply, go into our heart space, imagine moving higher and higher to our God-self and ask, "What is the thought I am creating that is bringing to me this lesson in illness?" The answer will come as a vision, a feeling, thought or knowingness. Once you realize what is occurring and why, you can heal or release the thought.

Exercise

Each day you can give yourself a "light examination." In other words, you can go through every part of your body to seek out any energy blocks that could create an illness, pain or trauma.

Sit quietly where you will not be disturbed. Imagine a crystal-clear flame of light in your heart. Place the flame within a tube that runs up and down in the center of your body. Inside the tube create two spirals, one moving clockwise and the other counterclockwise. Let the spirals of light move up and down and in and out.

Take your attention to the inside of your body, all the way down to your toes. Examine your toes on the energy level. Do you feel, see or sense any blockages in the forms of cloudiness, heaviness, or pain? If so, ask the energy to show you what is causing the blockage. Then release the thought into the spiral of light from your heart. See the blockage transmuted into love and light.

Move your attention through your legs, knees, thighs, hips, lower back, midsection, chest, shoulders, arms and hands, neck and head. Pay close attention to the areas of the joints. There are energy centers or chakras in every joint, and energy can often become trapped in these areas.

To release a block, simply focus your attention on the thought that is creating the block. Love and forgive yourself for holding onto the thought, acknowledge the thought, thanking it for its service in helping you learn a valuable lesson. Ask the thought to move from your body into the spiral where it is transmuted into love and light.

In examining the body in relation to thoughts and feelings, our feet relate to moving forward, in the right direction. Our legs and hips are our foundation, stability. Knees often reflect for us "bowing down" to others, or giving our power away instead of standing up for what we believe is right for us.

The lower back area reflects security issues, feeling we belong, that we are loved, that we have everything we need to be happy and healthy. Our shoulders reflect burdens or responsibilities we take on for ourselves or others.

Often we develop sore spots in the back of our neck where our neck joins the head. The head is the thinking part of us, the body is our feeling part. There are times we feel things we do not want to think about. And there are times we think about things we do not want to feel. In either case, the thoughts and feelings get stuck in our neck area and blockages of energy occur.

Do this exercise daily to maintain perfect health. Poor health is caused by imperfect thoughts. If we clear imperfect thoughts each day, they will not have time to establish themselves in our body. We will stay happy, healthy and loving.

AFFIRMATION: God and I are one. I was created in the image of God's perfection; therefore, I am perfect in all ways. I see myself as perfect. All that is not perfect is merely an illusion I have accepted as my truth. As I clear the illusion of imperfection, I stand in my power of perfection. I am whole. I am healthy. I am happy.

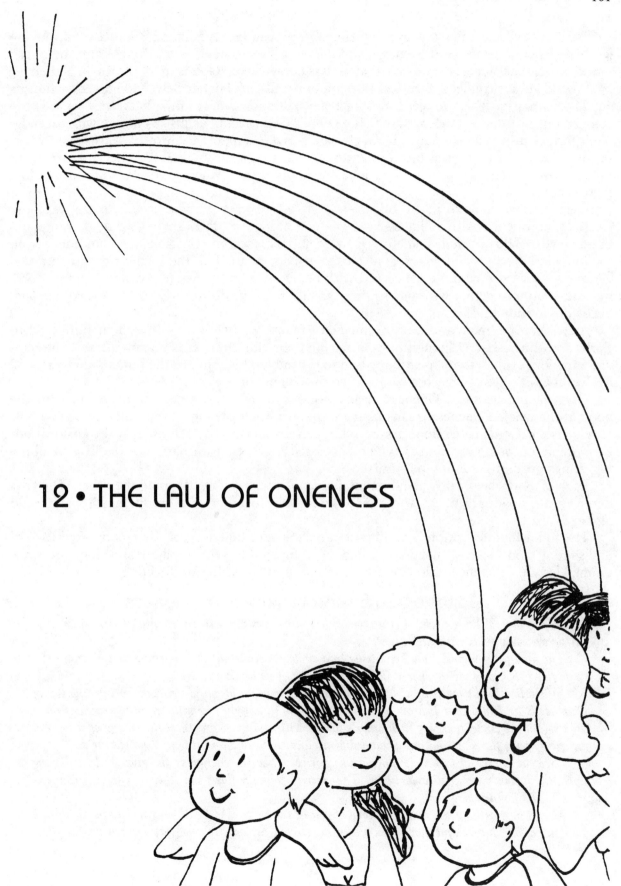

12 • THE LAW OF ONENESS

God is energy. Energy is everywhere. Energy can be visualized as an ocean of moving particles. Since God is energy and energy is everywhere, in all things from their very core of existence, we can say that God is everywhere. God is in all things, in all beings. We are always connected to God through our soul, our Higher Self. God loves each of us equally, no matter what we feel, think or believe about ourselves or others, how we act, the color of our skin, or whether we are rich or poor. God accepts us just as we are without judgment, criticism or punishment. Through God's loving support each of us learns the importance of seeing each other as brothers and sisters in God's spiritual family. Because we are all brothers and sisters, it is important to love one another, even when someone is not nice or loving toward us.

Each time we come to Earth to learn and grow in God's light, we become more and more aware of our oneness with all life everywhere. We become more aware of God in all things and in ourselves. Thus as we become more aware and expand our consciousness, our connection to God, God expands and grows. The closer we become to God, the higher we raise our own vibration. We become more concerned with being loving, positive, happy and helpful, working and sharing together with our spiritual family than we do in satisfying our own personal needs on an individual basis.

As we become more and more connected to God, we help bring more light from God to Earth and thus assist all living things in raising their vibration. It is a team effort. The mineral kingdom evolves to the plant kingdom to the animal kingdom to the human kingdom. All evolve in God's light to reach a common goal — divine oneness with God.

Oneness means unity. Oneness means working together as a community of one for the good of the whole. Oneness means taking responsibility for being all that one can be in a positive sense of God's perfection. As we take such responsibility, each of us will transform our own life in a positive way and in the process assist in the transformation of the lives of all living things on Earth and in God's universe.

Each of God's laws works hand in hand, one affecting and overlapping the other. The laws demonstrate how each of us works more effectively together as a group than separate and alone.

The following meditation is an important example of how we feel when connected to God and sharing God's love with all living things, as compared to being separate and alone. It is recommended that this meditation be done in a group, with facilitator directing the meditation.

Meditation on Separateness and Oneness

As a group, sit in a circle. Let everyone close their eyes and breathe deeply and rhythmically, letting the body relax with each breath.

The facilitator begins: "You are sitting in a circle. A circle has no beginning and no end. The circle flows as God's loving energy flows within each of us and without.

"Visualize God's love and light coming down as a beam of white light, down into the top of your heads and into your hearts. Imagine a beam of pink light extending from your heart, flowing around the circle, touching each other's hearts with loving energy. Feel the energy of the circle, an energy that flows on and on, around and around, with no beginning and no ending.

"See the energy of the circle flowing like a river. See the energy as the river of life, flowing smoothly, joyously, peacefully, lovingly. The river of your life flows smoothly as you stay connected to God's loving energy.

"I will now call out the names of some of you in the circle. As I call your names please release your neighbors' hands and move back out of the circle. Sit quietly and stay focused on your center."

[Note to facilitator: Call out every second, third or fourth person's name as you choose. This action will cause a disruption in the flow of the energy that has been created in the circle. Participants will then actually be able to feel the difference between being one with God and being separate.]

"Now feel the break in the flow of God's loving energy. Feel the disruption in the flow of your own life energy, the flow of your river. When we separate from God at any time, for any reason, we disrupt the flow of energy in our own bodies and our lives. We create disharmony, disease, dissatisfaction. We become angry, fearful, sad – even ill – when we separate from God.

"With our circle broken, focus now on bringing in God's love and light down through the top of your head, and from there out into your entire body. Expand this love and light until all you feel is God. Realize that even when you are separated from other people on Earth, from your friends and families, you are never truly separate from God. God is always with you. Feel the oneness – you and God.

Those of you who were called out of the circle, please move back into the circle and join hands with your neighbors. Bring God's love and light down through the top of your heads and into your hearts once more. Move the energy from your hearts down and out your arms and hands and all around the circle until all are once more connected. Feel God's loving light moving all around the circle, inside, outside, all around. Be one with this harmonious flow of God's love."

[Note: Ask participants to experience this energy flow for a moment, to go inside and be one with God. Then ask them to open their eyes when they feel ready.]

DISCUSSION

How do you feel when you are connected and flowing with God's loving energy? Discuss. How do you feel when you separate? Discuss.

For those of you who were asked to pull back from the circle, how did you feel about the experience? Discuss.

[Note to facilitator: Some participants may feel very lonely and abandoned, while others may not be disturbed by the break in the energy flow, which might mean they are more able to maintain a consistent awareness of God within themselves. This is the intent of this group lesson.]

We were created from the energy of God. Thus we can never truly be separate from God. We are here on Earth for learning experiences, and through the light of our soul we are ever connected to God. It is only the belief within the physical world, in our conscious mind, that makes us feel separate from God.

When we experience God within ourselves, we experience life as joyous, loving, peaceful, abundant, positive. By allowing our conscious mind to interfere with our relationship to God as being part of us, by accepting the thoughts, feelings and beliefs of others as our truth, or by listening to our own doubts and misconceptions, we might feel that God is not a part of us, that God does not love us, and in an extreme situation, that God does not exist, for if He/She did exist, there would not be so much disharmony on the Earth.

From the heart of divine love God created mankind and gave to each individual those qualities of Him/Herself that expressed goodness and love. God gave to mankind all that it would ever need to be happy, healthy and comfortable. At the time of creation, all was in balance and harmony, for that is how God planned the Earth experience.

The Earth experience was created for mankind to learn to balance the spiritual aspect with the dense, material world. Through God's gift of free will, mankind was given a choice to create whatever it wished on Earth. Although over a period of time mankind chose to feel separate from God and created its own little empire of material wealth on the Earth plane, it was and is always free to choose to follow God's laws.

How has mankind used its free will over the centuries? What has taken place? Discuss. How can we use our gift of free will to enhance the evolution of our soul? Discuss. [Note to facilitator: This discussion can include using our free will to connect with God; using our spiritual gifts to create God's world on Earth; using our free will to stay happy, healthy, loving and similar topics.]

Exercise

For this exercise you will need a large piece of butcher paper that can be taped to the wall for demonstration, and a marking pen.

Using the paper as a chart, ask the group to help list words that describe thoughts, feelings, emotions and actions that create separateness from God as well as oneness with God. If you are doing this exercise by yourself, you can simply list on a piece of paper those thoughts, feelings and emotions that create separateness and those that create oneness.

ENERGY OF SEPARATION	ENERGY OF ONENESS
Mine	Ours
Selfishness	Selflessness
Aloneness	Togetherness
Lack	Abundance
Fear	Faith
Illness	Health/wholeness
Doubt	Belief
Anger/hate	Unconditional love
Acting against God's laws	Working with God's laws

You can create two separate collages (groups) of pictures, words or phrases using magazine or newspaper clippings. Label one collage "My Feelings of Separateness from God" and the other "My Feelings of Oneness with God."

These collages can be as large or small as you wish to make them. Try to choose items for the collages that have a real impact and that could greatly impact those around you. Share your work with family and friends.

BUILDING BLOCKS TO GOD

As we examine the world in which we live, we find a great number of situations and circumstances that do anything but help us feel connected to God. There are those individuals who do not believe God exists. They express to others that if God did truly exist, the world would not be filled with such anger, hate, illness, poverty, starvation and the like.

As we look at our world, we find pollution of the water, the soil and the air. Many people in the world are starving and without water and medical care. There are severe diseases that doctors cannot find a cure for. Yet we know that God does exist, that God does care about us.

We must each remember that when we came to Earth we were given free will. Through free will we were offered an opportunity to follow God's laws and thus maintain total balance and harmony in our life and in the world, or to disobey God's universal laws and create our own experience separate from God. What we are seeing in the world today is humanity's choice to be separate from God and God's laws.

Each of us has the power to change what we do not like here on Earth. To do so, we must first change ourselves. As we change, we facilitate change in others. Like dominoes falling, one affects the next one.

To change, we must become aware of those qualities within us that are God-qualities and those that are not so that we can change them. We can see our God-qualities as building blocks, stairs leading back to God, our Creator.

The following exercise is offered to help you see just how many God-qualities you have within yourself and also those areas to be aware of that need assistance to represent God-qualities.

Exercise

Using a series of small boxes or shoe boxes, label the front of each box with the various qualities as we discuss them.

God is FEARLESS. Now look inside yourself. In how many different ways do you see yourself as fearless? If there are fears, what are you afraid of? Remember, fear is an absence of light. When you shine God's light on the fear, it dissolves. List those things you are not afraid of and put them into this box labeled "God Is Fearless."

God is LOVE. Look inside yourself and see in how many ways you display love toward yourself and others. If you do not feel love toward a particular individual or situation, look at the reason why you feel that way. Bring love down from God through the top of your head and out your heart center. Shine your love on that individual or situation. What happens? Be sure to write down the many ways you share God's love with yourself and others. Put the notes in the box labeled "God Is Love."

God is TRUTH. How many ways do you display truth? Do you always tell the truth? If not, why do you say things that are not true? Are you afraid of being punished? What would happen, do you think, if you told your parents the truth about something you felt they would punish you for? You may be surprised at how they lovingly accept your apology and not punish you if you tell the truth at all times. Be aware of the times you did not tell the truth. What happened? Now write down the number of ways you tell the truth and put them into the box marked, "God Is Truth."

God is POWER. Each of us is a part of God. Thus we can say that the power of God is within each of us equally. God-power does not control other people. It does not hurt other people. God-power merely allows each of us to stand up for our own truth, our own belief in what is right for us. How many times have you let someone talk you into doing something you felt was wrong? How did you feel about it? Were you afraid you would not be liked by your friend if you did not do what he/she wanted you to do? Remember, to be in God-power, you must stand up for what you feel is right. Sometimes it is better to let a friend go than to be a friend who is always used, taken advantage of and hurt in some way. Think of the number of ways you do not stand in your own power and forgive yourself for acting as you have. You have learned some important lessons any time you have given your God-power to others. Now look at all the ways you stand in your power and do what you know is right. Write them on a piece of paper and place the paper in the box marked "God Is Power."

There are many other qualities you can look for in yourself that are the qualities of God. For example, God is goodness, God is health, God is perfection, God is wisdom. God is limitless, God is forgiveness, God is light, God is energy, God is in me, God is all-knowing, God is everywhere and so on. Think of as many qualities as you can and follow the above exercise to make special note of those God-qualities within you. Pay close attention to the large number of qualities you already possess that make you feel one with God.

Connection with God in Meditation

When you pray, you talk to God. When you meditate, God talks to you. God is always awake, ready to listen to our needs and assist us to receive what we ask for. We simply need to ask for what we want and have faith that it will be provided.

Many times when we have a challenge in our life experience, we listen to family and friends to receive the answer. Many times, however, we do not find the answer outside of ourselves. In working with the Law of Oneness, we must remember that God is within each of us equally. Anytime we need to find a solution, we merely need to go inside ourselves.

The following exercise is a good way to practice talking to God, asking for answers.

Exercise

Think about a challenge in your life at the present time, anything that is causing your concern. Think about some of the answers you have received from your family and friends. You might want to list them on a piece of paper so you can remember more easily what was said.

Now focus on your question to God. Breathe and relax your body. Close your eyes and imagine yourself centered, grounded, protected in God's light.

Go deep within yourself to the center of your being, your heart. Imagine this spot as a beautiful crystal flame or light. Focus your attention on this light as it grows brighter and brighter and larger and larger.

Imagine a crystal-clear spiral of liquid light moving in a clockwise direction and another spiral of liquid light moving in a counterclockwise direction. Move the spiraling light energy upward as high as you can until you connect with the energy of God. You will feel this energy as very loving, very wise.

Look for your special place in the Godhead. There is one very special place within the energy of God that is your place and yours alone. Find that place and be there. Feel God's love all around you.

Focus on the challenge that you are faced with. Ask for a solution to the situation. Ask to see and understand clearly all that is taking place and what you are to learn from the experience. You will receive a message as a vision, a feeling, thought or a knowingness. Accept the first thing you feel, see or hear. This is your answer.

Whenever you seek answers from the God within you, you will always receive truth. When you listen to other people outside you, you will often receive messages that are clouded with other people's ideas, concepts and limiting beliefs. It is important to go inside and get your own answers. God is available to answer your call 24 hours a day.

The more you practice connecting to God through the spiral, feeling the oneness, the easier and more effortlessly you will move through your life experiences. Fewer situations will occur that you will not be able to handle quickly, without conflict, concern or worry.

AFFIRMATION: *I am thankful for the gift of life, for God's love and support. I affirm my oneness with God, with all of Creation. I take responsibility for myself and focus on creating harmony and balance within myself. What I am reflects out to all the world. I am love and light.*

CONCLUSION

From the heart of God came the love that created the universe, our Earth and all living things. From the mind of God came twelve very important universal laws which were designed to keep creation in balance and harmony. Each part of creation was given these laws and was shown how to apply them in their life experience. All parts of creation were in agreement except one — the human kingdom.

Free will has given humankind the opportunity to experiment with choice. The experiment has created separation from God, disease, discord, disharmony, imbalance. As the Earth begins to wither under the stress we have caused her, mankind has another choice: to continue to destroy the very foundation of life itself, or to reconnect with the God-energy, to surrender our free will to God's will and rebuild the Earth.

To accomplish the rebuilding project, we must release our rules, regulations, laws and requirements. We must surrender our old beliefs in favor of truth and light. We must begin to seek our answers, our requirements for life, from the very source of creation.

As we comprehend and begin to apply God's universal laws to our everyday life experiences, we begin to see positive change. Each law overlaps the others; not one law will stand alone without influencing or being influenced by another law. The laws are simple and easy to use and understand. Yet using these laws can make an incredible difference in how our life is or is not working.

Study the laws. Practice the exercises and meditations outlined in this book. Share the experience with family members and friends. Each day will bring you a new awareness, a new experience in joy, love, happiness, health and abundance. Through this new awareness all challenges will dissolve in light. Life on Earth will once again reflect the light and love as God created it to be. As one law cannot stand without the others, we too shall dissolve the separateness we created. We too shall know the importance of unity — one Family of Light.

BOOK MARKET

A reader's guide to the extraordinary books we publish, print and market for your enLightenment.

NEW!
THE EXPLORER RACE

Robert Shapiro/Zoosh

In this expansive overview, Zoosh explains, "You are the Explorer Race. Learn about your journey before coming to this Earth, your evolution here and what lies ahead." Topics range from ETs and UFOs to relationships.

the EXPLORER RACE
Zoosh, End-Time Historian through Robert Shapiro

$25.00 Softcover 650p   ISBN 0-929385-38-1

NEW!
ETs AND THE EXPLORER RACE

Robert Shapiro/Joopah

The next book in the famous Explorer Race series. Covers the Grays, abductions, the genetic experiment, UFO encounters, contactees, the future of our relationship with various ETs and much more.

ETs and the EXPLORER RACE
Joopah, Zoosh and others through Robert Shapiro

$14.95 softcover   ISBN 0-929385-79-9

BEHOLD A PALE HORSE

William Cooper

Former U.S. Naval Intelligence Briefing Team Member reveals information kept secret by our government since the 1940s. UFOs, the J.F.K. assassination, the Secret Government, the war on drugs and more by the world's leading expert on UFOs.

$25.00 Softcover 500p   ISBN 0-929385-22-5

◆ BOOKS BY LIGHT TECHNOLOGY RESEARCH

SHINING THE LIGHT

Revelations about the Secret Government and their connections with ETs. Information about renegade ETs mining the Moon, ancient Pleiadian warships, underground alien bases and many more startling facts.

$12.95 Softcover 208p   ISBN 0-929385-66-7

SHINING THE LIGHT BOOK II

Continuing the story of the Secret Government and alien involvement. Also information about the Photon Belt, cosmic holograms photographed in the sky, a new vortex forming near Sedona, and nefarious mining on sacred Hopi land.

$14.95 Softcover 422p   ISBN 0-929385-70-5

SHINING THE LIGHT BOOK III

The focus shifts from the dastardly deeds of the Secret Government to humanity's role in creation. The Earth receives unprecedented aid from Creator and cosmic councils, who recently lifted us beyond the third dimension to avert a great catastrophe.

$14.95 Softcover 512p   ISBN 0-929385-71-3

LIGHT TECHNOLOGY'S BOOKS OF LIGHT

THE SEDONA VORTEX GUIDEBOOK

by 12 channels

200-plus pages of channeled, never-before-published information on the vortex energies of Sedona and the techniques to enable you to use the vortexes as multidimensional portals to time, space and other realities.

$14.95 Softcover 236p   ISBN 0-929385-25-X

NEW!
THE ALIEN PRESENCE

Evidence of secret government contact with alien life forms.

Ananda

Documented testimony of the cover-up from a U.S. president's meeting with the tactics of suppression. The most complete information yet available.

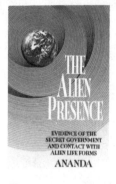

$19.95 Softcover   ISBN 0-929385-64-0

COLOR MEDICINE

The Secrets of Color Vibrational Healing

Charles Klotsche

A practitioner's manual for restoring blocked energy to the body systems with specific color wavelengths by the founder of "The 49th Vibrational Technique."

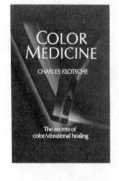

$11.95 Softcover 114p   ISBN 0-929385-27-6

◆ BOOKS BY DOROTHY ROEDER

THE NEXT DIMENSION IS LOVE

Ranoash

As speaker for a civilization whose species is more advanced, the entity describes the help they offer humanity by clearing the DNA. An exciting vision of our possibilities and future.

$11.95 Softcover 148p   ISBN 0-929385-50-0

REACH FOR US

Your Cosmic Teachers and Friends

Messages from Teachers, Ascended Masters and the Space Command explain the role they play in bringing the Divine Plan to the Earth now!

$14.95 Softcover 204p   ISBN 0-929385-69-1

CRYSTAL CO-CREATORS

A fascinating exploration of 100 forms of crystals, describing specific uses and their purpose, from the spiritual to the cellular, as agents of change. It clarifies the role of crystals in our awakening.

$14.95 Softcover 288p   ISBN 0-929385-40-3

BOOK MARKET

A reader's guide to the extraordinary books we publish, print and market for your enLightenment.

THE ASCENSION BOOK SERIES by JOSHUA DAVID STONE, Ph.D.

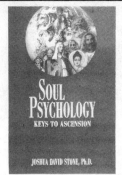

THE COMPLETE ASCENSION MANUAL

How to Achieve Ascension in This Lifetime

A synthesis of the past and guidance for ascension. An extraordinary compendium of practical techniques and spiritual history. Compiled from research and channeled information.

$14.95 Softcover 297p   ISBN 0-929385-55-1

SOUL PSYCHOLOGY

Keys to Ascension

Modern psychology deals exclusively with personality, ignoring the dimensions of spirit and soul. This book provides ground-breaking theories and techniques for healing and self-realization.

$14.95 Softcover 276p   ISBN 0-929385-56-X

BEYOND ASCENSION

How to Complete the Seven Levels of Initiation

Brings forth new channeled material that demystifies the 7 levels of initiation and how to attain them. It contains new information on how to open and anchor our 36 chakras.

$14.95 Softcover 279p   ISBN 0-929385-73-X

HIDDEN MYSTERIES

An Overview of History's Secrets from Mystery Schools to ET Contacts

Explores the unknown and suppressed aspects of Earth's past; reveals new information on the ET movement and secret teachings of the ancient Master schools.

$14.95 Softcover 333p   ISBN 0-929385-57-8

THE ASCENDED MASTERS LIGHT THE WAY

Keys to Spiritual Mastery from Those Who Achieved It

Lives and teachings of 40 of the world's greatest saints and spiritual beacons provide a blueprint for total self-realization. Guidance from those who mastered the secrets in their lifetimes.

$14.95 Softcover 258p   ISBN 0-929385-58-6

ASCENSION-ACTIVATION TAPES

How to anchor and open your 36 chakras and build your light quotient at a speed never dreamed possible. Scores of new ascension techniques and meditations directly from the galactic and universal core.

ASCENSION-ACTIVATION MEDITATION TAPE:

- S101
- S102
- S103   } $12.00 each
- S104
- S105

Set of all 5 tapes $49.95

LIGHT TECHNOLOGY'S BOOKS OF LIGHT

◆ BOOKS BY VYWAMUS/JANET McCLURE

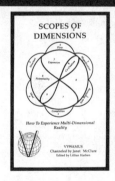

LIGHT TECHNIQUES

That Trigger Transformation

Expanding the Heart Center . . . Launching your Light . . . Releasing the destructive focus . . . Weaving a Garment of Light . . . Light Alignment & more. A wonderfully effective tool for using Light to transcend. Beautiful guidance!

$11.95 Softcover 145p   ISBN 0-929385-00-4

THE SOURCE ADVENTURE

Life is discovery, and this book is a journey of discovery "to learn, to grow, to recognize the opportunities – to be aware." It asks the big question, "Why are you here?" and leads the reader to examine the most significant questions of a lifetime.

$11.95 Softcover 157p   ISBN 0-929385-06-3

SCOPES OF DIMENSIONS

Vywamus explains the process of exploring and experiencing the dimensions. He teaches an integrated way to utilize the combined strengths of each dimension. It is a how-to guidebook for living in the multidimensional reality that is our true evolutionary path.

$11.95 Softcover 176p   ISBN 0-929385-09-8

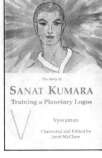

AHA! The Realization Book

w/ Lillian Harben

If you are mirroring your life in a way that is not desirable, this book can help you locate murky areas and make them "suddenly . . . crystal clear." Readers will find it an exciting step-by-step path to changing and evolving lives.

$11.95 Softcover 120p   ISBN 0-929385-14-4

SANAT KUMARA

Training a Planetary Logos

How was the beauty of this world created? The answer is in the story of Earth's Logos, the great being Sanat Kumara. A journey through his eyes as he learns the real-life lessons of training along the path of mastery.

$11.95 Softcover 179p   ISBN 0-929385-17-9

NEW! COCREATOR UNIVERSITY

Vywamus, Djwhal Khul & Atlanto

Your four bodies, the Tibetan Lesson series, the Twelve Rays, the Cosmic Walk-in and others. All previously unpublished channelings by Janet McClure.

$14.95 Softcover   ISBN 0-929385-54-3

COCREATOR UNIVERSITY

Vywamus, Djwhal Khul, The Tibetan, and Atlanto
Channeled by Janet McClure

BOOK MARKET

A reader's guide to the extraordinary books we publish, print and market for your enLightenment.

◆ BOOKS BY LYNN BUESS

CHILDREN OF LIGHT, CHILDREN OF DENIAL

In his fourth book Lynn calls upon his decades of practice as counselor and psychotherapist to explore the relationship between karma and the new insights from ACOA/ Co-dependency writings.

$8.95 Softcover 150p   ISBN 0-929385-15-2

NUMEROLOGY FOR THE NEW AGE

An established standard, explicating for contemporary readers the ancient art and science of symbol, cycle, and vibration. Provides insights into the patterns of our personal lives. Includes life and personality numbers.

$11.00 Softcover 262p   ISBN 0-929385-31-4

NUMEROLOGY: NUANCES IN RELATIONSHIPS

Provides valuable assistance in the quest to better understand compatibilities and conflicts with a significant other. A handy guide for calculating your/his/her personality numbers.

$12.65 Softcover 239p   ISBN 0-929385-23-3

THE STORY OF THE PEOPLE
Eileen Rota

An exciting history of our coming to Earth, our traditions, our choices and the coming changes, it can be viewed as a metaphysical adventure, science fiction or the epic of all of us brave enough to know the truth. Beautifully written and illustrated.

$11.95 Softcover 209p   ISBN 0-929385-51-9

THE NEW AGE PRIMER
Spiritual Tools for Awakening

A guidebook to the changing reality, it is an overview of the concepts and techniques of mastery by authorities in their fields. Explores reincarnation, belief systems and transformative tools from astrology to crystals.

$11.95 Softcover 206p   ISBN 0-929385-48-9

LIVING RAINBOWS
Gabriel H. Bain

A fascinating "how-to" manual to make experiencing human, astral, animal and plant auras an everyday event. Series of techniques, exercises and illustrations guide the reader to see and hear aural energy. Spiral-bound workbook.

$14.95 Softcover 134p   ISBN 0-929385-42-X

LIGHT TECHNOLOGY'S BOOKS OF LIGHT

ACUPRESSURE FOR THE SOUL
Nancy Fallon, Ph.D.

A revolutionary vision of emotions as sources of power, rocket fuel for fulfilling our purpose. A formula for awakening transformation with 12 beautiful illustrations.

$11.95 Softcover 150p   ISBN 0-929385-49-7

◆ BOOKS BY RUTH RYDEN

THE GOLDEN PATH

"Book of Lessons" by the master teachers explaining the process of channeling. Akashic Records, karma, opening the third eye, the ego and the meaning of Bible stories. It is a master class for opening your personal pathway.

$11.95 Softcover 200p   ISBN 0-929385-43-8

LIVING THE GOLDEN PATH
Practical Soul-utions to Today's Problems

Guidance that can be used in the real world to solve dilemmas, to strengthen inner resolves and see the Light at the end of the road. Covers the difficult issues of addictions, rape, abortion, suicide and personal loss.

$11.95 Softcover 186p   ISBN 0-929385-65-9

◆ BOOKS BY WES BATEMAN

KNOWLEDGE FROM THE STARS

A telepath with contact to ETs, Bateman has provided a wide spectrum of scientific information. A fascinating compilation of articles surveying the Federation, ETs, evolution and the trading houses, all part of the true history of the galaxy.

$11.95 Softcover 171p   ISBN 0-929385-39-X

DRAGONS AND CHARIOTS

An explanation of spacecraft, propulsion systems, gravity, the Dragon, manipulated Light and interstellar and intergalactic motherships by a renowned telepath who details specific technological information received from ETs.

$9.95 Softcover 65p   ISBN 0-929385-45-4

FOREVER YOUNG
Gladys Iris Clark

You can create a longer younger life! Viewing a lifetime of a full century, a remarkable woman shares her secrets for longevity and rejuvenation. A manual for all ages. Explores tools for optimizing vitality, nutrition, skin care via Tibetan exercises, crystals, sex.

$9.95 Softcover 109p   ISBN 0-929385-53-5

BOOK MARKET

A reader's guide to the extraordinary books we publish, print and market for your enLightenment.

ANNOUNCING a CHILDREN'S DIVISION — STARCHILD PRESS

CACTUS EDDIE
Brian Gold

Imaginative and colorful, charmingly illustrated with 20 detailed paintings by the artist author. The tale of a small boy who when separated from his family has more adventures than Pecos Bill. Printed in large 8½" by 11" format. A beautiful book!

$11.95 Softcover 62p   ISBN 0-929385-74-8

THE GREAT KACHINA
Lou Bader

A warm, delightful story that will help children understand Kachina energy. With 20 full-color illustrations, printed in 8½" by 11" format to dramatize the artwork.

$11.95 Softcover 62p   ISBN 0-929385-60-8

IN THE SHADOW OF THE SAN FRANCISCO PEAKS
Lou Bader

Collection of tales about those who shaped the frontier and were changed by it. A young boy's experiences with people and the wilderness is fascinating reading for all ages.

$9.95 Softcover 152p   ISBN 0-929385-52-7

SPIRIT OF THE NINJA
Toni Siegel

Returning as a dog, a Spiritual Warrior gains love and peace with a young woman in Sedona. Profoundly moving tale for all ages.

$7.95 Softcover 67p   ISBN 0-9627746-0-X

SONG OF SIRIUS
Dorothy McManus

A truthful view of modern teens who face drugs and death, love and forgiveness. Guided by Eckrita of Sirius, they each find their destiny and desires.

$8.00 Softcover 155p   ISBN 0-929686-01-2

I WANT TO KNOW
Aloa Starr

Inspiring responses to the questions of Why am I here? Who is God? Who is Jesus? What do dreams mean? and What do angels do? Invites contemplation, sets values and delights the young.

$7.00 Softcover 87p   ISBN 0-929686-02-0

LIGHT TECHNOLOGY'S BOOKS OF LIGHT

◆ THE LITTLE ANGEL BOOKS by LEIA STINNETT

A CIRCLE OF ANGELS
A workbook. An in-depth teaching tool with exercises and illustrations throughout.
$18.95 ISBN 0-929385-87-X

THE 12 UNIVERSAL LAWS
A workbook for all ages. Learning to live the Universal Laws; exercises and illustrations throughout.
$18.95 ISBN 0-929385-81-0

WHERE IS GOD?
Story of a child who finds God in himself and teaches others.
$4.95 ISBN 0-929385-90-X

HAPPY FEET
A child's guide to foot reflexology, with pictures to guide.
$4.95 ISBN 0-929385-88-8

WHEN THE EARTH WAS NEW
Teaches ways to protect and care for our Earth.
$4.95 ISBN 0-929385-91-8

THE ANGEL TOLD ME TO TELL YOU GOODBYE
Near-death experience heals his fear.
$4.95 ISBN 0-929385-84-5

COLOR ME ONE
Lessons in competition, sharing and separateness.
$4.95 ISBN 0-929385-82-9

ONE RED ROSE
Explores discrimination, judgment, and the unity of love.
$4.95 ISBN 0-929385-83-7

WHO'S AFRAID OF THE DARK?
Fearful Freddie learns to overcome with love.
$4.95 ISBN 0-929385-89-6

THE BRIDGE BETWEEN TWO WORLDS
Comfort for the "Star Children" on Earth.
$4.95 ISBN 0-929385-85-3

EXPLORING THE CHAKRAS
Ways to balance energy and feel healthy.
$4.95 ISBN 0-929385-86-1

CRYSTALS FOR KIDS
Workbook to teach care and properties of stones.
$4.95 ISBN 0-929385-92-6

BOOK MARKET

A reader's guide to the extraordinary books we publish, print and market for your enLightenment.

◆ BOOKS by HALLIE DEERING

LIGHT FROM THE ANGELS
Channeling the Angel Academy

Now those who cannot attend the Angel Academy in person can meet the Rose Angels who share their metaphysical wisdom and technology in this fascinating book.

$15.00 Softcover 230p   ISBN 0-929385-72-1

DO-IT-YOURSELF POWER TOOLS

Assemble your own glass disks that holographically amplify energy to heal trauma, open the heart & mind, destroy negative thought forms, tune the base chakra and other powerful work. Build 10 angelic instruments worth $700.

$25.00 Softcover 96p   ISBN 0-929385-63-2

PRISONERS OF EARTH
Psychic Possession and Its Release
Aloa Starr

The symptoms, causes and release techniques in a documented exploration by a practitioner. A fascinating study that demystifies possession.

$11.95 Softcover 179p   ISBN 0-929385-37-3

◆ RICHARD DANNELLEY

SEDONA POWER SPOT, VORTEX AND MEDICINE WHEEL GUIDE

Discover why this book is so popular! Six detailed maps, special meditations for each power spot, and a lot of heart. Richard Dannelley is a native of the Sedona area.

$11.00 Softcover 112p   ISBN 0-9629453-2-3

NEW!
SEDONA: BEYOND THE VORTEX
The Ultimate Journey to Your Personal Place of Power

An advanced guide to ascension, using vortex power, sacred geometry, and the Merkaba.

$12.00 Softcover 152p   ISBN 0-9629453-7-4

THIS WORLD AND THE NEXT ONE
Aiello

A handbook about your life before birth and your life after death, it explains the how and why of experiences with space people and dimensions. Man in his many forms is a "puppet on the stage of creation."

THIS WORLD AND THE NEXT ONE

(AND THERE IS A NEXT ONE)

By "AIELLO"

(This Is About Your Life Before Birth and Your Life After Death)

A Handbook of How and Why!

$9.95 Softcover 213p   ISBN 0-929385-44-6

LIGHT TECHNOLOGY'S BOOKS OF LIGHT

◆ BOOKS by TOM DONGO

NEW!
MERGING DIMENSIONS
with Linda Bradshaw

The authors' personal experiences. 132 photographs of strange events, otherworldly beings, strange flying craft, unexplained light anomalies. *They're leaving physical evidence!*

$14.95 Softcover 200p   ISBN 0-9622748-4-4

UNSEEN BEINGS UNSEEN WORLDS

Venture into unknown realms with a leading researcher. Discover new information on how to communicate with nonphysical beings, aliens, ghosts, wee people and the Gray zone. Photos of ET activity and interaction with humans.

$9.95 Softcover 122p   ISBN 0-9622748-3-6

THE LEGEND OF THE EAGLE CLAN
Cathleen M. Cramer with Derren A. Robb

The emotionally charged story of Morning Glory, a remembrance of her life 144 years ago as part of the Anasazi, the ancient ones. This book is for those who need to remember who they are.

$12.95 Softcover 281p   ISBN 0-929385-68-3

THE ALIEN TIDE
The Mysteries of Sedona II

UFO/ET events and paranormal activity in the Sedona area and U.S. are investigated by a leading researcher who cautions against fear of the alien presence. For all who seek new insights. Photos/illustrations.

$7.95 Softcover 128p   ISBN 0-9622748-1-X

THE QUEST
The Mysteries of Sedona III

Fascinating in-depth interviews with 26 who have answered the call to Sedona and speak of their spiritual experiences. Explores the mystique of the area and effect the quests have had on individual lives. Photos/illustrations.

$8.95 Softcover 144p   ISBN 0-9622748-2-8

THE MYSTERIES OF SEDONA

An overview of the New Age Mecca that is Sedona, Arizona. Topics are the famous energy vortexes, UFOs, channeling, Lemuria, metaphysical and mystical experiences and area paranormal activity. Photos/illustrations.

$6.95 Softcover 84p   ISBN 0-9622748-0-1

Book Market

A reader's guide to the extraordinary books we publish, print and market for your enLightenment.

✦ BOOKS by ROYAL PRIEST RESEARCH

PRISM OF LYRA

Traces the inception of the human race back to Lyra, where the original expansion of the duality was begun, to be finally integrated on earth. Fascinating channeled information.

$11.95 Softcover 112p   ISBN 0-9631320-0-8

VISITORS FROM WITHIN

Explores the extra-terrestrial contact and abduction phenomenon in a unique and intriguing way. Narrative, precisely focused channeling & firsthand accounts.

$12.95 Softcover 171p   ISBN 0-9631320-1-6

PREPARING FOR CONTACT

Contact requires a metamorphosis of consciousness, since it involves two species who meet on the next step of evolution. A channeled guidebook to ready us for that transformation. Engrossing.

$12.95 Softcover 188p   ISBN 0-9631320-2-4

SOUL RECOVERY & EXTRACTION

Ai Gvhdi Waya

Soul recovery is about regaining the pieces of one's spirit that have been trapped, lost or stolen either by another person or through a traumatic incident that has occurred in one's life.

$9.95 Softcover 74p   ISBN 0-9634662-3-2

I'M O.K. I'M JUST MUTATING!

The Golden Star Alliance

Major shifts are now taking place upon this planet. It is mutating into a Body of Light, as are all the beings who have chosen to be here at this time. A view of what is happening and the mutational symptoms you may be experiencing.

$6.00 Softcover 32p

OUR COSMIC ANCESTORS

Maurice Chatelain

A former NASA expert documents evidence left in codes inscribed on ancient monuments pointing to the existence of an advanced prehistoric civilization regularly visited (and technologically assisted) by ETs.

$9.95 Softcover 216p   ISBN 0-929686-00-4

LIGHT TECHNOLOGY'S BOOKS OF LIGHT

✦ BOOKS by PRESTON NICHOLS with PETER MOON

THE MONTAUK PROJECT

Experiments in Time

The truth about time that reads like science fiction! Secret research with invisibility experiments that culminated at Montauk, tapping the powers of creation and manipulating time itself. Exposé by the technical director.

$15.95 Softcover 156p   ISBN 0-9631889-0-9

MONTAUK REVISITED

Adventures in Synchronicity

The sequel unmasks the occult forces that were behind the technology of Montauk and the incredible characters associated with it.

$19.95 Softcover 249p   ISBN 0-9631889-1-7

PYRAMIDS OF MONTAUK

Explorations in Consciousness

A journey through the mystery schools of Earth unlocking the secret of the Sphinx, thus awakening the consciousness of humanity to its ancient history and origins.

$19.95 Softcover 249p   ISBN 0-9631889-2-5

ENCOUNTER IN THE PLEIADES:

An Inside Look at UFOs

For the first time, the personal history of Preston Nichols is revealed, also amazing information the world has not yet heard. An unprecedented insight into the technology of flying saucers. Never has the complex subject of UFOs been explained in such simple language.

$19.95 Softcover   ISBN 0-9631889-3-3

ACCESS YOUR BRAIN'S JOY CENTER

Pete Sanders Jr.

An M.I.T.-trained scientist's discovery of how to self-trigger the brain's natural mood-elevation mechanisms as an alternative to alcohol, nicotine, drugs or overeating to cope with life's pressures and challenges. Combination book and audio cassette package.

$29.95 Softcover 90p plus tape   ISBN 0-9641911-0-5

PRINCIPLES TO REMEMBER AND APPLY

Maile

A handbook for the heart and mind, it will spark and expand your remembrance. Explores space, time, relationships, health and includes beautiful meditations and affirmations. Lucid and penetrating.

$11.95 Softcover 114p   ISBN 0-929385-59-4

BOOK MARKET

A reader's guide to the extraordinary books we publish, print and market for your enLightenment.

ORDER NOW!
1-800-450-0985
or Fax 1-800-393-7017
Or use order form at end

NEW!
A Dedication to the SOUL/SOLE GOOD OF HUMANITY
Maria Vosacek

DEDICATED TO THE SOUL/SOLE GOOD OF HUMANITY

MARIA VOSACEK

To open awareness, the author shares information drawn from looking beyond the doorway into the Light. She explores dreams, UFOs, crystals, relationships and ascension.

$9.95 Softcover 288p   ISBN 0-9640683-9-7

SEDONA STARSEED
Raymond Mardyks

There is a boundary between the dimensions humans experience as reality and the beyond. Voices from beyond the veil revealed a series of messages. The stars and constellations will guide you to the place inside where infinite possibilities exist.

$14.95 Softcover 146p   ISBN 0-9644180-0-2

EARTH IN ASCENSION
Nancy Anne Clark, Ph.D.

EARTH IN ASCENSION

About the past, present and future of planet Earth and the role humans will play in her progress. Nothing can stop Earth's incredible journey into the unknown. You who asked to participate in the birthing of Gaia into the fifth dimension were chosen!

$14.95 Softcover 136p   ISBN 0-9648307-6-0

WE ARE ONE:
A Challenge to Traditional Christianity
Ellwood Norquist

We Are One:
A Challenge to Traditional Christianity
By Ellwood Norquist

Is there a more fulfilling way to deal with Christianity than by perceiving humankind as sinful, separate and in need of salvation? Humanity is divine, one with its Creator, and already saved.

$14.95 Softcover 169p   ISBN 0-9646995-2-4

AWAKEN TO THE HEALER WITHIN
Rich Work & Ann Marie Groth

Awaken To The Healer Within
by Rich Work with Ann Marie Groth

An empowerment of the soul, an awakening within and a releasing of bonds and emotions that have held us tethered to physical and emotional disharmonies. A tool to open the awareness of your healing ability.

$14.95 Softcover 330p   ISBN 0-9648002-0-9

TEMPLE OF THE LIVING EARTH
Nicole Christine

Temple of the Living Earth

Nicole Christine
Crystal Priestess of Gaia

An intimate true story that activates the realization that the Living Earth is our temple and that we are all priests and priestesses to the world. A call to the human spirit to celebrate life and awaken to its cocreative partnership with Earth.

$16.00 Softcover 150p   ISBN 0-9647306-0-X

LIGHT TECHNOLOGY'S BOOKS OF LIGHT

THE ONLY PLANET OF CHOICE
Council of Nine through Phyllis V. Schlemmer

"A PROVOCATIVE MIND-OPENING EXPERIENCE"
The Only Planet of Choice
Essential Briefings from Deep Space
Phyllis V. Schlemmer

One of the most significant books of our time, updated. About free will and the power of Earth's inhabitants to create a harmonious world. Covers ET civilizations, the nature of the Source of the universe, humanity's ancient history etc.

$14.95 Softcover 342p   ISBN 1-85860-023-5

INANNA RETURNS
V.S. Ferguson

INANNA RETURNS
V.S. Ferguson

A story of the gods and their interaction with humankind. Simple tale by Inanna, whose Pleiadian family, including Enlil and Enki, took over the Earth 500,000 years ago, this story brings the gods to life as real beings with problems and weaknesses, although technologically superior.

$14.00 Softcover 274p

IT'S TIME TO REMEMBER
Joy S. Gilbert

It's Time To Remember
A Riveting Story of One Woman's Awakening to Alien Beings
By Joy S. Gilbert

A riveting story of one woman's awakening to alien beings. Joy recounts her initial sightings, dreams and ongoing interaction with nonhuman beings she calls her friends. After her terror, she sees her experiences as transformative and joyful.

$19.95 Hardcover 186p   ISBN 0-9645941-4-5

✦ MAGICAL SEDONA through the DIDGERIDOO by TAKA

Magical Sedona through the Didgeridoo

Taka blends the sound of the Didgeridoo into the sacred landscape of Sedona, Arizona, describing different areas, joining with the characteristic animal and nature sounds he has experienced and recorded over the years. The drone of the Didgeridoo takes us into a state between conscious and unconscious; the joy of nature sounds and the human voice touches deeper levels in our beings and we are reconnected with all creation. Each selection is approximately 10 minutes long and starts and ends at sunrise. The music will give you, wherever you are, the opportunity to tune in to the magic of Sedona.

1. *Cathedral Rock* • Nurturing, beauty
2. *Bell Rock* • Energizing, guardian
3. *Dry Beaver Creek* • Inspiring, creative
4. *Airport* • Direction beyond limitation
5. *Canyons* • Sheltering, motherly
6. *Sedona* • Love

T101 $12.00

LIFE ON THE CUTTING EDGE
Sal Rachelle

LIFE ON THE CUTTING EDGE

SAL RACHELLE

The most significant questions of our time require a cosmic view of reality. From the evolution of consciousness, dimensions and ETs to the New World Order, this is a no-nonsense book from behind and beyond the scenes. A must-read!

$14.95 Softcover 336p   ISBN 0-9640535-0-0

BOOK MARKET

A reader's guide to the extraordinary books we publish, print and market for your enLightenment.

ARCTURUS PROBE
José Argüelles

A poetic depiction of how the Earth was seeded by beings from the Arcturus system of three million years ago. The author of *The Mayan Factor* tells how Atlantis and Elysium were played out on Mars and implanted into Earth consciousness. Illustrated.

$14.95 Softcover   ISBN 0-929385-75-6

GUARDIANS OF THE FLAME
Tamar George

Channeled drama of a golden city in a crystal land tells of Atlantis, the source of humanity's ritual, healing, myth and astrology. Life in Atlantis over 12,000 years ago through the eyes of Persephone, a magician who can become invisible. A story you'll get lost in.

$14.95 Softcover   ISBN 0-929385-76-4

THE MILLENNIUM TABLETS
John McIntosh

Twelve tablets containing 12 powerful secrets, yet only 2 opened. The Light-bearers and Way-showers will pave the way, dispelling darkness and allowing the opening of the 10 remaining tablets to humanity, thus beginning the age of total freedom.

$14.95 Softcover   ISBN 0-929385-78-0

THE TRANSFORM-ATIVE VISION
José Argüelles

Reprint of his 1975 tour de force, which prophesied the Harmonic Convergence as the "climax of matter," the collapse of materialism. Follows the evolution of the human soul in modern times by reviewing its expressions through the arts and philosophers.

$14.95 Softcover 364p   ISBN 0-9631750-0-9

OUT-OF-BODY EXPLORATION
Jerry Mulvin

Techniques for traveling in the Soul Body to achieve absolute freedom and experience truth for oneself. Discover reincarnation, karma and your personal spiritual path.

$8.95 Softcover 87p   ISBN 0-941464-01-6

VOICES OF SPIRIT
Charles H. Hapgood

The author discusses 15 years of work with Elwood Babbit, the famed channel. Will fascinate both the curious sceptic and the believer. Includes complete transcripts.

$13.00 Softcover 350p   ISBN 1-881343-00-6

LIGHT TECHNOLOGY'S BOOKS OF LIGHT

KRYON – Book I
The End Times
Kryon through Lee Carroll

New information for **personal peace.** Valuable metaphysical material presented in a simple easy-to-read manner.

$12.00 Softcover   ISBN 0-9636304-2-3

KRYON – Book II
Don't Think Like a Human
Kryon through Lee Carroll

Channeled answers to basic questions. Leading to a new way of being, which will allowing miracles to come into one's life.

$12.00 Softcover   ISBN 0-9636304-0-7

KRYON – Book III
Alchemy of The Human Spirit
Kryon through Lee Carroll

A guide to human transition into the New Age. Book III of the Kryon books covers predictions, validations, skeptics, science, mathematics and more. Two special appendices on the mysterious 9944 math.

$14.00 Softcover 376p   ISBN 0-9636304-8-2

TOUCHED BY LOVE
Dorothy McManus

From the exotic jungles of the Congo to New York's Fifth Avenue, this story sweeps the reader along in a fast-moving adventure of suspense, passion and romance. A strong theme of faith in the Universe is woven throughout the book.

$9.95 Softcover 191p   ISBN 0-929686-03-9

POISONS THAT HEAL
Eileen Nauman DHM (UK)

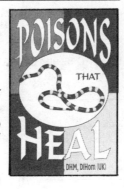

Homeopathy is all that remains to protect us from the deadly superbugs and viruses that modern medicine has failed to turn back. Learn how to protect yourself and your family against the coming Ebola virus and other deadly diseases.

$14.95 Softcover 270p   ISBN 0-929385-62-4

PEACE LABYRINTH
Sacred Grometry
Dr. Beatrice Bartnett

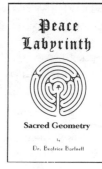

The author explains the meaning and significance of the Peace Labyrinth, a sacred geometry space. Using the numberology of the ancient Egyptians, the book explores ways of connecting with God, balancing energy, celebrations and exercises.

$9.95 Softcover 56p   ISBN 0-9622182-7-8

BOOKS PUBLISHED BY LIGHT TECHNOLOGY PUBLISHING

			No. Copies	Total
Acupressure for the Soul	Fallon	$11.95	____	$_____
Alien Presence	Ananda	$19.95	____	$_____
Arcturus Probe	Argüelles	$14.95	____	$_____
Behold a Pale Horse	Cooper	$25.00	____	$_____
Cactus Eddie	Gold	$11.95	____	$_____
Channelling	Vywamus/Burns	$ 9.95	____	$_____
Color Medicine	Klotsche	$11.95	____	$_____
ETs and the Explorer Race	Shapiro	$14.95	____	$_____
Explorer Race	Shapiro	$25.00	____	$_____
Forever Young	Clark	$ 9.95	____	$_____
Guardians of The Flame	George	$14.95	____	$_____
Great Kachina	Bader	$11.95	____	$_____
Legend of the Eagle Clan	Cramer	$12.95	____	$_____
Living Rainbows	Bain	$14.95	____	$_____
Mahatma I & II	Grattan	$19.95	____	$_____
Millennium Tablets	McIntosh	$14.95	____	$_____
New Age Primer		$11.95	____	$_____
Poisons That Heal	Nauman	$14.95	____	$_____
Prisoners of Earth	Starr	$11.95	____	$_____
Sedona Vortex Guide Book		$14.95	____	$_____
Shadow of San Francisco Peaks	Bader	$ 9.95	____	$_____
The Soul Remembers	Warter	$14.95	____	$_____
Story of the People	Rota	$11.95	____	$_____
This World and the Next One	Aiello	$ 9.95	____	$_____

LIGHT TECHNOLOGY RESEARCH/FANNING
Shining the Light		$12.95	____	$_____
Shining the Light — Book II		$14.95	____	$_____
Shining the Light — Book III		$14.95	____	$_____

ARTHUR FANNING
Souls, Evolution & the Father		$12.95	____	$_____
Simon		$ 9.95	____	$_____

WESLEY H. BATEMAN
Dragons & Chariots		$ 9.95	____	$_____
Knowledge From the Stars		$11.95	____	$_____

LYNN BUESS
Children of Light, Children of Denial		$ 8.95	____	$_____
Numerology: Nuances in Relationships		$12.65	____	$_____
Numerology for the New Age		$11.00	____	$_____

RUTH RYDEN
		No. Copies	Total
The Golden Path	$11.95	____	$_____
Living The Golden Path	$11.95	____	$_____

DOROTHY ROEDER
Crystal Co-Creators	$14.95	____	$_____
Next Dimension is Love	$11.95	____	$_____
Reach For Us	$14.95	____	$_____

HALLIE DEERING
Light From the Angels	$15.00	____	$_____
Do-It-Yourself Power Tools	$25.00	____	$_____

JOSHUA DAVID STONE, PH.D.
Complete Ascension Manual	$14.95	____	$_____
Soul Psychology	$14.95	____	$_____
Beyond Ascension	$14.95	____	$_____
Hidden Mysteries	$14.95	____	$_____
Ascended Masters	$14.95	____	$_____

VYWAMUS/JANET MCCLURE
AHA! The Realization Book	$11.95	____	$_____
Light Techniques	$11.95	____	$_____
Sanat Kumara	$11.95	____	$_____
Scopes of Dimensions	$11.95	____	$_____
The Source Adventure	$11.95	____	$_____
Evolution: Our Loop of Experiencing	$14.95	____	$_____

LEIA STINNETT
A Circle of Angels	$18.95	____	$_____
The Twelve Universal Laws	$18.95	____	$_____
Where Is God?	$ 4.95	____	$_____
Happy Feet	$ 4.95	____	$_____
When the Earth Was New	$ 4.95	____	$_____
The Angel Told Me To Tell You Goodby	$ 4.95	____	$_____
Color Me One	$ 4.95	____	$_____
One Red Rose	$ 4.95	____	$_____
Exploring the Chakras	$ 4.95	____	$_____
Crystals For Kids	$ 4.95	____	$_____
Who's Afraid of the Dark	$ 4.95	____	$_____
The Bridge Between Two Worlds	$ 4.95	____	$_____

BOOKS PRINTED OR MARKETED BY LIGHT TECHNOLOGY PUBLISHING

			No. Copies	Total
Access Your Brain's Joy Center (w/ tape)	Sanders	$29.95	____	$_____
Awaken to the Healer Within	Work, Groth	$14.95	____	$_____
A Dedication to the Soul/Sole. . .	Vosacek	$ 9.95	____	$_____
Earth in Ascension	Clark	$14.95	____	$_____
God Within	Free	$11.95	____	$_____
"I'm OK I'm Just Mutating"	Golden Star Alliance	$ 6.00	____	$_____
Innana Returns	Ferguson	$14.00	____	$_____
It's Time To Remember	Gilbert	$19.95	____	$_____
I Want To Know	Starr	$ 7.00	____	$_____
Life On the Cutting Edge	Rachelle	$14.95	____	$_____
Look Within	Free	$9.95	____	$_____
Medical Astrology	Nauman	$29.95	____	$_____
Our Cosmic Ancestors	Chatelain	$ 9.95	____	$_____
Out-Of-Body Exploration	Mulvin	$ 8.95	____	$_____
Peace Labyrinth	Bartnett	$ 9.95	____	$_____
Principles To Remember and Apply	Maile	$11.95	____	$_____
Sedona Starseed	Mardyks	$14.95	____	$_____
Song of Sirius	McManus	$ 8.00	____	$_____
Soul Recovery and Extraction	Waya	$ 9.95	____	$_____
Spirit of The Ninja	Siege	$ 7.95	____	$_____
Temple of The Living Earth	Christine	$16.00	____	$_____

			No. Copies	Total
The Only Planet of Choice	Schlemmer	$14.95	____	$_____
Touched By Love	McManus	$ 9.95	____	$_____
We Are One	Norquist	$14.95	____	$_____

Richard Dannelley
Sedona Power Spot/Guide	$11.00	____	$_____
Sedona: Beyond The Vortex	$12.00	____	$_____

Tom Dongo: Mysteries of Sedona
Mysteries of Sedona — Book I	$ 6.95	____	$_____
Alien Tide—Book II	$ 7.95	____	$_____
Quest—Book III	$ 8.95	____	$_____
Unseen Beings, Unseen Worlds	$ 9.95	____	$_____
Merging Dimensions	$14.95	____	$_____

Preston B. Nichols with Peter Moon
Montauk Project	$15.95	____	$_____
Montauk Revisited	$19.95	____	$_____
Pyramids of Montauk	$19.95	____	$_____
Encounter in the Pleiades: Inside Look at UFOs	$19.95	____	$_____

Lyssa Royal and Keith Priest
Preparing For Contact	$12.95	____	$_____
Prism of Lyra	$11.95	____	$_____
Visitors From Within	$12.95	____	$_____

ASCENSION MEDITATION TAPES

JOSHUA DAVID STONE, PH.D.
Ascension Activation Meditation	S101	$12.00	____	$_____
Tree of Life Ascension Meditation	S102	$12.00	____	$_____
Mt. Shasta Ascension Activation Meditation	S103	$12.00	____	$_____
Kabbalistic Ascension Activation	S104	$12.00	____	$_____
Complete Ascension Manual Meditation	S105	$12.00	____	$_____
Set of all 5 tapes		$49.95	____	$_____

VYWAMUS/BARBARA BURNS
The Quantum Mechanical You (6 tapes)	B101-6	$40.00	____	$_____

TAKA
Magical Sedona through the Didgeridoo	T101	$12.00	____	$_____

BRIAN GRATTAN
Seattle Seminar Resurrection 1994 (12 tapes)	M102	$79.95	____	$_____

YHWH/ARTHUR FANNING
On Becoming	F101	$10.00	____	$_____
Healing Meditations/Knowing Self	F102	$10.00	____	$_____
Manifestation & Alignment w/ Poles	F103	$10.00	____	$_____
The Art of Shutting Up	F104	$10.00	____	$_____
Continuity of Consciousness	F105	$25.00	____	$_____
Black-Hole Meditation	F106	$10.00	____	$_____
Merging the Golden Light Replicas of You	F107	$10.00	____	$_____

BOOKSTORE DISCOUNTS HONORED

❏ CHECK ❏ MONEY ORDER

CREDIT CARD: ❏ MC ❏ VISA

\# _____

Exp. date:_____

Signature:_____

(U.S. FUNDS ONLY) PAYABLE TO:

LIGHT TECHNOLOGY PUBLISHING

P.O. BOX 1526 • SEDONA • AZ 86339
(520) 282-6523 FAX: (520) 282-4130

1-800-450-0985
Fax 1-800-393-7017

NAME/COMPANY_____

ADDRESS_____

CITY/STATE/ZIP_____

PHONE_____ CONTACT_____

SUBTOTAL: $_____

SALES TAX: $_____
(7.5% - AZ residents only)

SHIPPING/HANDLING: $_____
('3 Min.; 10% of orders over '30)

CANADA S/H: $_____
(20% of order)

TOTAL AMOUNT ENCLOSED: $_____

All prices in US$. Higher in Canada and Europe.

CANADA: DEMPSEY (604) 683-5541 FAX (604) 683-5521 • ENGLAND/EUROPE: WINDRUSH PRESS LTD. 0608 652012/652025 FAX 0608 652125
AUSTRALIA: GEMCRAFT BOOKS (03) 888-0111 FAX (03) 888-0044 • NEW ZEALAND: PEACEFUL LIVING PUB. (07) 571-8105 FAX (07) 571-8513